Ethnic minorities in the labour market

Ethnic minorities in the labour market

Dynamics and diversity

Ken Clark and Stephen Drinkwater

JOSEPH ROWNTREE
FOUNDATION

First published in Great Britain in 2007 by

The Policy Press
Fourth Floor, Beacon House
Queen's Road
Bristol BS8 1QU
UK

Tel no   +44 (0)117 331 4054
Fax no   +44 (0)117 331 4093
Email   tpp-info@bristol.ac.uk
www.policypress.org.uk

© University of Manchester 2007

Transferred to Digital Print 2008

Published for the Joseph Rowntree Foundation by The Policy Press

ISBN 978 1 86134 959 0

British Library Cataloguing in Publication Data
A catalogue record for this book is available from the British Library.

Library of Congress Cataloging-in-Publication Data
A catalog record for this book has been requested.

Ken Clark is a senior lecturer in economics at the University of Manchester, UK, and **Stephen Drinkwater** is a senior lecturer in economics at the University of Surrey. Both authors are research fellows of the Institute for the Study of Labor (IZA) in Bonn, Germany.

The **Joseph Rowntree Foundation** has supported this project as part of its programme of research and innovative development projects, which it hopes will be of value to policy makers, practitioners and service users. The facts presented and views expressed in this report are, however, those of the authors and not necessarily those of the Foundation.

Cover design by Qube Design Associates, Bristol
Printed in Great Britain by Marston Book Services, Oxford.

Contents

List of figures

List of tables

Acknowledgements

We are grateful to Kathleen Kelly of the Joseph Rowntree Foundation for her help and advice. We would also like to thank the members of the advisory group for their extremely useful comments throughout the duration of the project. The support of the Office for National Statistics, the General Register Office for Scotland, the Northern Ireland Statistical Research Agency, the CCSR (Cathie Marsh Centre for Census and Survey Research) and the ESRC/JISC (Economic and Social Research Council/Joint Information Systems Committee) Census of Population Programme is gratefully acknowledged. Census output is Crown copyright and is reproduced with the permission of the Controller of HMSO and the Queen's Printer for Scotland. The authors alone are responsible for the interpretation of the data. Further information on the Census microdata used in this report is available at www. ccsr.ac.uk/sars.

Members of the advisory group

Professor David Blackaby, Department of Economics, University of Wales Swansea

Professor Angela Dale OBE, CCSR, University of Manchester

Dr David Drew, Department for Work and Pensions

Professor Derek Leslie, Department of Economics, Manchester Metropolitan University

Mr Stephen Munn, Department for Work and Pensions

Dr Ludi Simpson, CCSR, University of Manchester

Summary

Different ethnic minorities have diverse labour market experiences. Some groups such as the Chinese and Indians fare relatively well, while others such as the Pakistanis and Bangladeshis do worse. We examine the experiences of ethnic minorities in detail to establish the nature and extent of ethnic diversity in the UK labour market. To achieve this, we principally use Census microdata as these provide us with large enough samples to analyse each of the ethnic groups and also enable us to examine the impact of local area effects. Furthermore, the 2001 microdata contain better information than previous years on educational qualifications and also asked a question on religion for the first time, both of which are important factors in driving employment outcomes for ethnic groups.

Our second focus is on changes in the labour market outcomes of ethnic groups over the 1990s. Given the far healthier labour market that prevailed in 2001 compared with 1991, we investigate whether disadvantaged ethnic minorities benefited from this overall improvement in job opportunities. When making comparisons over time we mainly focus on the differences between six ethnic minorities (Black Caribbeans, Black Africans, Indians, Pakistanis, Bangladeshis, Chinese) and the White group. The main labour market outcomes under scrutiny are employment, self-employment and occupational attainment.

We argue that employment is a key indicator of welfare and that employment rates that exclude students are the most appropriate way to measure this. It is found that there was a relative improvement in the employment performance of most ethnic minorities between 1991 and 2001. The largest improvements were experienced by Black African, Pakistani and Bangladeshis men – which could partly be explained by the increased levels of education within these groups. The degree of convergence with the White group was smaller for ethnic minority women, with the Pakistani and Bangladeshi groups continuing to have very low employment rates. Religion is likely to explain some of this – although it is difficult in this context to disentangle the effects of religion and ethnicity. Nevertheless, Muslim women have significantly lower employment rates across a range of ethnic groups. The factors influencing employment rates are also ethnically diverse: education has a large positive impact on employment rates, with the effects especially large for ethnic minorities. There are also differential effects of local area deprivation – or neighbourhood effects – by ethnic group.

Self-employment is an important form of economic activity for ethnic minority men in Britain and we find that over time there was some convergence in self-employment rates between groups. In particular, the Chinese and Indian groups had lower rates of self-employment in 2001 compared with 1991. We argue that this is consistent with second-generation Chinese and Indians choosing not to follow their parents into business and instead finding employment in the paid labour market. In contrast, Pakistanis and Bangladeshis experienced no such decline in self-employment rates despite having similar demographic characteristics.

There is little evidence of occupational progress among ethnic minorities between 1991 and 2001 when other factors such as education are taken into account. The only group to experience much advancement was Black Caribbean men. Higher education graduates also appear to be finding it increasingly difficult to obtain professional or managerial jobs, with this tendency greatest for women, especially Black Caribbeans and Black Africans. Using Labour Force Survey data, wide earnings deficits relative to the White group continue to be observed for ethnic minority men in particular. The largest differentials are experienced by Black Africans, Pakistanis and Bangladeshis and the lowest by the Chinese, Black Caribbeans and Indians. Within occupation, the largest earnings gaps are observed for managerial and professional workers, suggesting that ethnic minorities find it difficult to obtain high-ranking executive positions.

A number of policy conclusions emerge from our results:

- Ethnic diversity needs to be taken seriously when setting policy targets in the labour market and when designing policies. Such policies need to be targeted to specific ethnic groups and be sensitive to their needs.
- Education is the key building block of labour market success for all groups and this offers the opportunity for government policy to improve the employment prospects of disadvantaged groups, particularly Black Caribbean men, where drop-out rates are highest.
- Although religion appears to exert an important influence on labour market outcomes, this is a complicated area for policy makers and one where further research is needed. However, the situation of some groups (for example, Muslims) could be improved with targeted resources and greater sensitivity towards certain aspects of tradition and culture, such as in the provision of childcare and job-search assistance.
- The differential impact of local socioeconomic conditions by ethnic group suggests a targeted approach to policy making in this area, although further research and better data are required to establish the precise causal mechanisms involved.
- Our findings suggest that the quality as well as quantity of self-employment among ethnic minorities is important and policy must reflect this.
- Labour market discrimination is apparently deep-rooted, widespread and persistent. There may be scope for the introduction of more interventionist, anti-discrimination policies in the workplace.

Introduction

The welfare of ethnic minorities has received increased attention in recent years, partly because of the rising proportion of the UK population accounted for by individuals from ethnic minority communities and partly due to issues connected to social cohesion. This has led to a growing interest by government policy makers in the welfare of ethnic minority individuals. This report focuses on an important determinant of welfare, namely labour market performance. In particular, two intertwined themes are investigated. First, the labour market outcomes of the UK's largest ethnic minorities are very different. For example, members of the Indian and Chinese communities perform relatively well in terms of occupational attainment, earnings and employment in comparison with the White majority group, whereas Pakistanis and Bangladeshis fare much worse (Leslie et al, 1998). Thus, the project will analyse in detail the **diversity** of ethnic minority labour market experience. The second key theme concerns changes over time in the absolute and relative labour market status of ethnic minorities. Research has found that the relative labour market positions of ethnic groups are not constant through time. In particular, changes in discrimination between decades have been detected (Blackaby et al, 1994, 2002) and business cycles have different effects on ethnic minorities compared with the White group (Leslie et al, 2002). Thus, the report will provide a detailed investigation of the **dynamics** of labour market performance within and between Britain's ethnic minorities over the 1990s.

Census of the Population data will principally be used to examine ethnic differences in a variety of labour market outcomes. In particular, Census microdata from 1991 and 2001 will inform the majority of our analysis. The use of such datasets, known as the Individual Samples of Anonymised Records (SARs), offers a number of advantages. First, only Census microdata offer the large sample sizes that are necessary to treat ethnic diversity seriously. Establishing differences in labour market outcomes between different ethnic groups requires more observations from these groups than are typically available in other datasets such as the Labour Force Survey (LFS). It is especially important to have access to relatively large samples, given the need to conduct statistical analysis on men and women separately – since different factors will impact on labour market decisions for women compared with men. Second, microdata based on the Census records of individuals allow the researcher to control (in a statistical model) for observable characteristics when examining differences between ethnic groups. This is crucial in determining whether differences in average labour market outcomes between groups are due to changes in the average productive characteristics of the groups, including human capital, or whether they cannot be ascribed to observable characteristics and are therefore due to other factors, including discriminatory treatment in the labour market. Finally, Census microdata allow more flexibility than aggregate data, which is vital when there is a need to examine the situation of particular subgroups of the population. For example, labour market data for ethnic groups using aggregate information from the 2001 Census are only reported for two age groups – 16-24 and 25-74 – and thus do not map very easily into the working-age population.

From the perspective of making comparisons across time, it is important to have a consistent measure of certain key concepts and Appendix A contains some discussion of this. At this juncture it is worth noting that there have been changes in the questions that have been asked in the Census and in the way in which the data have been released between 1991 and 2001. For example, in 2001 the Census contained more detailed information on ethnicity, education and religion. Furthermore, in 2001 a special file, known as the Individual Controlled Access Microdata Sample (CAMS), was made available to researchers for analysis only at Office for National Statistics (ONS) sites. This file contains more detailed information on a wider range of variables than is available in the individual licensed version of the 2001 SAR.[1] Furthermore, the CAMS contains local authority identifiers – allowing the location of individuals to be known at a sub-regional level of geography – and the Index of Multiple Deprivation, which measures the general level of economic and social deprivation in an individual's neighbourhood. This is particularly useful when analysing ethnic minorities in the UK because of the regional and local concentrations of particular ethnic minorities and the varying labour market performance of individuals in these areas (Clark and Drinkwater, 2002; Simpson et al, 2006).[2] In the subsequent analysis we make use of the 1991 SARs as well as the 2001 SARs and CAMS. We also supplement the analysis with data from recent sweeps of the LFS, where these yield additional insights.

It is also useful to consider the definition of ethnic group used in this analysis. The question on ethnicity changed between the two Censuses, with a more detailed question asked in 2001. This allowed for the separate identification of groups among the White community as well as permitting individuals to be identified as members of a range of mixed race groups. Since much of our work compares the situation of ethnic minorities across time, we require a definition of ethnicity that is relatively constant across the period. To achieve this, we make use of the studies by Simpson and Akinwale (2004) and ONS (2006), which exploit the Longitudinal Study (LS) of England and Wales to examine changes in individuals' reported ethnicity between 1991 and 2001.[3] Both studies find that there are seven clearly defined groups that are relatively stable over the period – White, Black Caribbean, Black African, Indian, Pakistani, Bangladeshi and Chinese, although the two Black groups were the most likely to have problems of consistency over the period. Thus, we focus on these seven groups (plus a catch-all Other category) in our comparisons of employment in 1991 and 2001 microdata. The more detailed 2001 classification is used in some analyses to provide extra information.

Overview

To conclude this chapter, we put the forthcoming analysis into context by briefly describing the broader labour market situation in the UK over the period in question. It is important to note that the labour market had improved considerably in 2001 compared with 1991 when the UK was still in recession. For example, the unemployment rate in the UK fell from 8.6% in 1991 to 5.0% in 2001, which was far better than the improvement in the Organisation for Economic Co-operation and Development (OECD) as a whole, where unemployment only fell from 6.8% to 6.5% (OECD, 2003). Furthermore between 1992 and 2001, the UK economy created more than a million new jobs and real Gross Domestic Product growth averaged 2.8%. It might be thought that this relatively favourable economic climate would lead to brighter labour market prospects, both in terms of employment

---

[1] Examples include the full coding of age in the CAMS compared with the 2001 Individual Licensed SAR, which only contains ages in discrete categories and a much finer disaggregation of country of birth.

[2] One other point to note is that if the analysis requires the microdata from 1991 and 2001 to be combined, the 2001 SARs need to be used, given that the 1991 SARs are not available at ONS sites. Therefore, both the CAMS and 2001 SARs will be used in this report.

[3] The LS contains, inter alia, information on the Census returns for the same individuals for approximately 1% of the population of England and Wales since 1971.

and success at work. The extent to which such an improvement has actually occurred for different ethnic groups will be a key aspect of this report.

To introduce some of the most important trends for the different ethnic groups we consider in this report, Figures A and B report the distribution of individuals of working age across different labour market states in both 1991 and 2001, Figure A for men and Figure B for women. For each ethnic group the pie charts report the proportion of the working-age population in our sample who are in paid-employment, self-employment, unemployed or inactive.

It is clear from the figures that there is considerable diversity in labour market status by ethnicity and gender. Focusing on men first, White, Indian and the Chinese groups had relatively low proportions of the working-age population unemployed in 1991, while the Black, Pakistani and Bangladeshi groups faced much higher unemployment. Over time the proportion in employment grew, with corresponding reductions in unemployment for all ethnic groups. It is also noticeable that inactivity increased for all groups. Finally, the high proportion in self-employment for the Pakistani, Bangladeshi, Indian and Chinese groups is evident, although this fell somewhat over the period for the latter two groups.

For women there is quite a different pattern. Not only is self-employment a negligible form of activity for most groups except the Chinese, inactivity unsurprisingly accounts for much higher proportions. This is particularly the case for the Pakistani and Bangladeshi groups where at least 65% of the working-age population are classified as inactive in both years. Employment has grown for these groups over the period as it has for every single group. In contrast to men, employment growth has occurred at the same time as increasing labour market activity.

This brief overview of the UK labour market during this period emphasises the importance of jointly considering the diversity and dynamics of ethnic minority labour market experience. Different groups have diverse outcomes and, even within groups, gender differences can be considerable. Nor is the pattern of diversity constant over time: the direction of change for individual groups or by gender cannot be predicted by examining the behaviour of the average individual as this average is dominated by the White group. The remainder of the report attempts to untangle some these patterns and trends.

Organisation of the report

In the following chapters we will focus on three key aspects of the labour market performance of ethnic minorities. First, since employment is a key determinant of welfare, Chapter 2 examines the dynamics and diversity of employability across different ethnic groups over the period 1991-2001. Second, reflecting the importance of self-employment to some ethnic groups, Chapter 3 explores the changing patterns of ethnic entrepreneurship. Chapter 4 concentrates on workplace success by considering occupational attainment and earnings. As indicated above, each of these chapters focuses not only on ethnic diversity in labour market outcomes but also on the changes that have occurred over time. Separate analysis by gender is also conducted where feasible. Finally, Chapter 5 contains conclusions and policy implications.

Figure A: Ethnic minorities in the labour market

Males 1991 and 2001

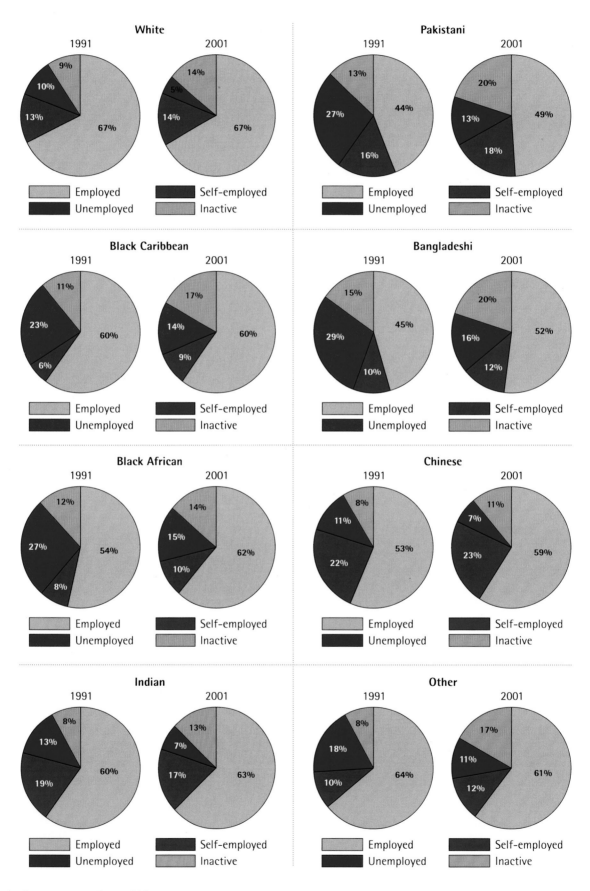

Source: 1991 and 2001 SARs

Figure B: Ethnic minorities in the labour market

Females 1991 and 2001

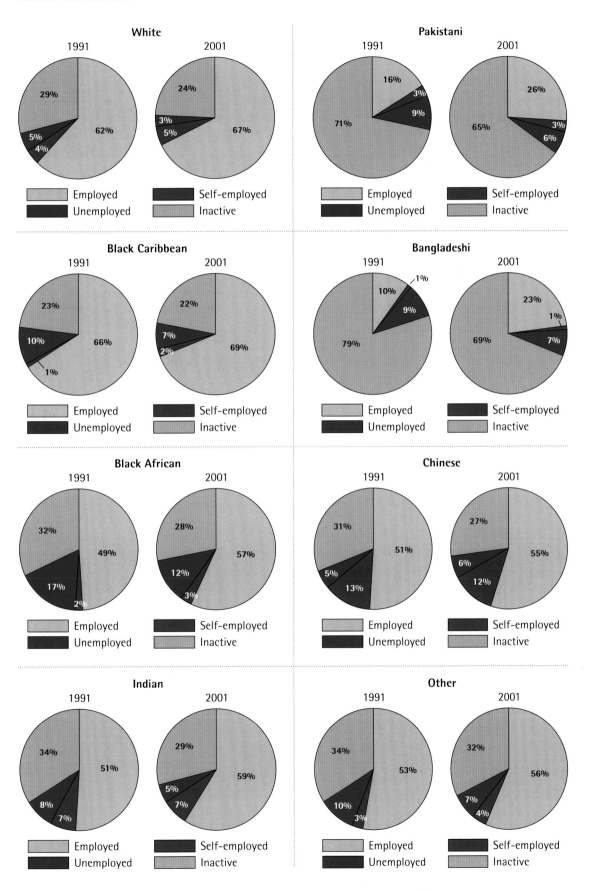

Source: 1991 and 2001 SARs

2

Employment

Perhaps the biggest influence on an individual's welfare is whether or not they have a job, even if this is a low-paid position. There are several reasons for this. First, those out of work report lower levels of general well-being than those with jobs and this can lead to problems with their mental and physical health (Clark and Oswald, 1994). Second, a strong link has been established between being out of work and poverty. In particular, families with an out-of-work parent have a significantly increased chance of falling below the poverty line (Blanden and Gibbons, 2006). Third, jobless individuals often experience what are known as scarring effects (Arulampalam et al, 2001). This refers to the phenomenon whereby a period of unemployment can reduce the chances of an individual subsequently finding a job due to the attrition of human capital or because employers screen out those with past unemployment spells. Finally, higher levels of unemployment have also been associated with an increasing incidence of crime and social disruption (Freeman, 1999). Therefore, improving the employment prospects of different population subgroups, including those from ethnic minority communities, has become an important issue for government.

It is important to measure employment outcomes appropriately and issues surrounding the best measure to use when analysing the labour market performance of ethnic minorities will be discussed later in this chapter. Most measures are based on employment rates, defined as the ratio of those in employment (either paid or self-employment) to the population of working age. These are the focus of the UK government's labour market policies through its endorsement of the European Union's Lisbon Agenda and the UK government's strategy to improve the labour market position of ethnic minorities uses the employment rate as the key indicator of success (DWP, 2001, 2004). The employment rate is also the complement of 'worklessness', a measure that has gained influence in recent years (Gregg and Wadsworth, 2004). Worklessness has been identified as one of the leading correlates of poverty in the UK (Nickell, 2004).

Employment rates are known to vary along a number of dimensions; however, up until the recession of the 1980s, there were relatively small ethnic employment differences in the UK. For example, Smith (1976), using the National Survey of Ethnic Minorities, reported that West Indian and Asian men experienced unemployment rates of less than 3% in the early 1970s, similar to those of White men at that time,[4] although much larger ethnic differences were observed in terms of female employment rates. Even in the early 1980s, Brown (1984) was unable to find substantial ethnic employment differences among men – employment rates for West Indian and Asian men were 64% and 68% respectively, compared with 67% for White men, a difference of 2-3 percentage points. However, unemployment rose among ethnic minorities in the 1980s and this continued in the 1990s. Blackaby et al (1994), using General Household Survey (GHS) data, reported that the employment disadvantage suffered by ethnic minority men compared with White men leapt from 2.6 percentage points in the 1970s to 10.9 percentage points in the 1980s.

---

[4] Leslie et al (2002) make the same point on the basis of time series data.

The availability of the 1991 Samples of Anonymised Records (SARs) meant that employment outcomes could be explored for a much wider set of ethnic groups, as well as separately by gender. For example, Blackaby et al (1997) analysed employment differences between the White group and nine ethnic minorities and established that Black African, Pakistani and Bangladeshi groups were particularly prone to unemployment. In contrast, it was found that the Chinese and Indian groups experienced very similar unemployment rates to the White group. However, this study focused only on unemployment, whereas it may be more meaningful to investigate employment differences more generally because of the low rates of economic activity among some ethnic minorities, especially Pakistani and Bangladeshi women (Holdsworth and Dale, 1997), and increasingly among older men (Disney, 1999). Furthermore, individuals from most ethnic minorities are much more likely than White groups to stay on in post-compulsory education (Drew, 1995; Leslie and Drinkwater, 1999). Therefore, these issues will be borne in mind when considering which is the most appropriate measure to use when analysing ethnic differences in labour market activity.

The importance of labour market definitions

Table 1 reports measures of labour market activity for the 10 ethnic groups that could be identified in the 1991 SARs. The four labour market categories that are included in the table are activity rates, employment rates, employment rates (excluding students) and unemployment rates.[5] Table 2 reports these labour market measures for the 16 ethnic groups identifiable from the 2001 Census. The information for 1991 is taken from the SARs, while for 2001, the source is the Controlled Access Microdata Sample (CAMS).[6] Both tables relate only to England and Wales. Scotland and Northern Ireland have been excluded because different ethnicity questions were asked in these countries in 2001 and we want to examine the full extent of ethnic diversity on as consistent a basis as possible.[7]

It can be seen from Table 1 that there was considerable ethnic diversity in labour market outcomes in 1991. The most noticeable features are the extremely low activity rates of Pakistani and Bangladeshi women and the very high levels of unemployment experienced by some ethnic groups, both for men and women. In particular, over a quarter of economically active men from the three Black groups, as well as Pakistani and Bangladeshi men and women, were unemployed in 1991, while the unemployment rate of Black African women was just under 25%. In comparison, the unemployment rates for White men and women were 10.9% and 6.5% respectively. The only ethnic minority to experience similar levels of unemployment to White people in 1991 was the Chinese group, while jobless rates among the Indian and Other Asian groups were somewhat higher.

Given the higher activity rates of men, the main factor driving the low employment rates of men in 1991 was the high level of unemployment at this time, while for women low employment rates seem to have been the result of a combination of both high rates of

---

[5] See Appendix A for details of how these rates have been constructed from Census responses. Appendix A also contains a discussion of how ethnicity was defined in 1991 and 2001.

[6] The main reason for using the CAMS is because it contains a richer set of factors that can be used in the subsequent regressions, for example, full detail on age, country of birth and more narrowly defined spatial identifiers.

[7] There are also differences in the religion question asked in these two countries and in the education question asked in Scotland in 2001. Moreover, the ethnic minority population in each of these countries is small, with 2.01% of the Scottish and 0.75% of the Northern Irish populations from the ethnic minorities in 2001. Both of these amounts are lower than the percentage of ethnic minorities in the Welsh population (2.14%). 9.08% of residents in England were from the ethnic minority communities in 2001, ranging from 2.31% in the South West to 28.86% in London.

Table 1: Labour market outcomes by ethnic group, England and Wales: 1991

	Male				Female			
	Activity rate	Employment rate	Employment rate (no students)	Unemployment rate	Activity rate	Employment rate	Employment rate (no students)	Unemployment rate
White	86.1	76.8	81.1	10.9	67.3	62.9	67.0	6.5
Black Caribbean	84.7	63.4	66.8	25.1	72.3	63.1	67.9	12.7
Black African	64.8	45.8	62.6	29.4	56.2	42.4	52.2	24.6
Black Other	82.9	60.6	67.9	26.9	64.6	52.8	60.5	18.3
Indian	81.4	69.8	78.8	14.2	59.1	51.7	57.9	12.6
Pakistani	73.7	50.8	59.7	31.0	26.6	18.6	20.8	30.3
Bangladeshi	73.1	48.5	56.4	33.7	20.0	12.4	14.1	38.1
Chinese	65.9	58.4	81.6	11.5	53.1	49.3	64.4	7.1
Other Asian	74.1	63.3	79.6	14.6	53.4	46.7	54.0	12.6
Other Other	77.5	62.2	73.4	19.7	56.3	48.5	58.5	13.8

Source: 1991 Census, SARs. © Crown copyright

Note: Sample size relates to working-age population (16-59/64). All figures are percentages.

Table 2: Labour market outcomes by ethnic group, England and Wales: 2001

	Male				Female			
	Activity rate	Employment rate	Employment rate (no students)	Unemployment rate	Activity rate	Employment rate	Employment rate (no students)	Unemployment rate
White British	82.5	77.8	81.2	5.7	72.2	69.1	72.0	4.2
White Irish	76.1	71.0	73.4	6.8	70.4	67.0	69.5	4.9
Other White	76.5	71.2	80.6	7.0	65.4	61.2	67.9	6.4
Mixed: White & Black Caribbean	73.7	60.7	68.8	17.6	62.0	53.2	60.1	14.2
Mixed: White & Black African	70.9	55.4	64.0	21.8	60.2	54.3	60.6	9.8
Mixed: White & Asian	70.9	64.2	77.5	9.4	62.2	57.1	65.2	8.2
Other Mixed	69.6	61.1	73.6	12.2	61.6	55.6	65.1	9.8
Indian	77.4	71.3	80.6	7.9	63.7	59.2	65.2	7.2
Pakistani	68.0	57.0	66.4	16.2	31.0	25.4	27.4	18.0
Bangladeshi	68.6	54.7	63.3	20.3	27.9	21.4	22.2	23.0
Other Asian	72.2	64.5	73.6	10.7	54.9	49.8	55.7	9.3
Black Caribbean	77.5	64.5	68.9	16.8	72.8	66.1	71.0	9.3
Black African	71.7	59.2	72.0	17.4	60.1	50.0	58.8	16.8
Other Black	72.5	58.7	67.8	19.1	66.9	57.0	64.2	14.7
Chinese	64.8	60.1	82.4	7.3	56.7	52.4	66.7	7.7
Other	63.6	55.7	71.3	12.4	52.1	47.4	55.5	9.0

Source: 2001 Census, CAMS. © Crown copyright

Note: Sample size relates to working-age population (16–59/64). All figures are percentages.

inactivity and unemployment. The clearest example of the latter is the Pakistani and Bangladeshi groups where these factors combine to produce employment rates of well under 20% for each of these groups. Female employment rates were also less than 50% for Black Africans, Chinese, Other Asians and Others. For the Chinese, low employment rates are in large part explained by the high proportion in post-compulsory education. This can be seen by comparing the conventional employment rate with the employment rate that excludes students, since when students are removed the employment rate rises to almost 65%, similar to that of White women. The highest employment rate (with and without students) among women was achieved by the Black Caribbean group, despite this group having an unemployment rate almost double that of the White group in 1991.

For men, the discrepancy between employment rates with and without students was also largest for the Chinese. Furthermore, when students are excluded the employment rate for Chinese men exceeded that of White men in 1991. The difference between the two employment rates was also considerable for Black African men (17 percentage points) and was 8 percentage points or more for Indian, Pakistani and Bangladeshi men, compared with just under 4 percentage points for White men.

Despite the general reduction in unemployment rates over the 1990s, Table 2 shows that male unemployment rates were still in excess of 10% in 2001 for all ethnic minorities apart from the Chinese, Indian and the Mixed: White & Asian groups. Furthermore, unemployment rates were in excess of 20% for Bangladeshi men and men identifying themselves as Mixed: White & Black African. The employment rates of some of the Mixed groups are particularly low, with just over a half of Mixed: White & Black Africans in employment and less than two thirds of this group in employment even after the exclusion of students. White Britons had the highest employment rate of the White groups, with White Irish men experiencing relatively low levels of employment after the exclusion of students. The table again shows the importance of excluding students from the employment rate. For example, the employment rate discrepancy when students were excluded was in excess of 10 percentage points for the Chinese, Black African, Mixed: White & Asian, Other and Other Mixed men. For Chinese men, the exclusion of students implies that they have the highest employment rate. However, even after the removal of students, relatively low employment rates were still observed in 2001 for Pakistani and Bangladeshi men.

The overall situation for women was slightly better, with only five out of the 13 ethnic minorities recording an unemployment rate in excess of 10% in 2001. Some interesting anomalies are also observed for the Mixed groups, with Mixed: White & Black Caribbean women experiencing the lowest employment rate among the Mixed groups despite the high employment rates for the White and Black Caribbean groups individually, while the Mixed: White & Asian group had the highest rate out of all of the Mixed and Other groups even though some of the Asian groups experience very low levels of employment. The factors underlying the employment rates of the mixed ethnicity groups are complex. For example, the social and cultural implications of belonging to, or declaring, a mixed ethnicity are likely to be important (Mansaray, 2003), as may be the respective social classes of the parents of mixed ethnicity individuals.

Pakistani and Bangladeshi women continued to have very low economic activity rates between 1991 and 2001 and this, combined with the continued high levels of unemployment, produced employment rates for these groups of less than 30% in 2001, even after the exclusion of students. The comparable employment rates for White and Black Caribbean women were over 70% after the exclusion of students.

In the subsequent econometric analysis we focus on the employment rate where full-time students are removed from the numerator and denominator. We choose to focus on employment rates because of the patterns that we have observed both for 1991 and 2001. In particular, as we saw in Figures A and B in Chapter 1, there is a large amount of inactivity among certain groups, especially Pakistani and Bangladeshi women and increasingly for older men. As a result, a comparison of unemployment rates would fail to take account of the economically inactive. Students are excluded since, compared with White individuals, people from many of the ethnic minorities are more likely to stay on in post-compulsory education, deferring their labour market entry in anticipation of enhanced future earnings and employment opportunities.[8] Because the vast majority of students are labour market inactive, the inclusion of students would reduce the employment rate considerably for some ethnic minorities.

Before moving on to a more detailed exploration of ethnic differences using Census microdata, it is useful to compare the information provided by the 2001 CAMS with that available from the most recently available data from the Labour Force Survey (LFS). To enable this comparison, Table A1 in Appendix C contains the sample sizes and employment rates (excluding students) for 15 ethnic groups using the CAMS and pooled LFS surveys from 2002 to 2005.[9] The first point to notice from the table is that despite combining 16 quarters of LFS data, the sample sizes from the CAMS are much larger. For some groups, such as the mixed groups, the sample size in the CAMS is up to six times as great as that available in the LFS. Subject to the caveat that smaller sample sizes are likely to increase sampling error, Table A1 suggests that the general increase in employment rates for men tended to continue for most ethnic groups after 2001. Encouragingly, the employment rates for Black Caribbean, Black African, Pakistani and Bangladeshi men have increased by more than 3 percentage points since the last Census. The picture for women is less favourable, since employment rates fell for all of the main ethnic minorities, whereas they increased for the White group. This further emphasises the driving force of unemployment for male employment rates and the influence of other factors for female employment rates.

Decomposing the employment gap: 1991 and 2001

Figures C to F show the results of decomposing the employment gap with the White group for each of the six comparable ethnic groups for men and women in 1991 and 2001. The gap is decomposed into two effects: a characteristics and a coefficients component. The characteristics component refers to the amount of the employment gap that can be explained by the variables that have been included in a probit regression model.[10] As a result, this effect is also known as the explained effect. The other component, known as the coefficients or unexplained effect, reflects all other influences on employment that vary, on average, between groups. This may include labour market discrimination but it would be incorrect to ascribe all of this effect to discrimination as this would assume that all employment-enhancing characteristics have been included in the model.[11]

---

[8]   Full-time students are also removed from the numerator in 2001, since some are recorded as economically active. Please see Appendix A for further details.

[9]   The White Irish category is not available in the LFS. Sixteen quarters of LFS data have been combined to achieve reasonable sample sizes for the smaller ethnic groups. Only those individuals in their first wave of interviews have been included in the sample to avoid double counting.

[10] See Appendix B for further details of the decomposition technique. The variables included in the model needed to be available in both 1991 and 2001, which constrains the possible empirical specifications. Controls were included for age, marital status, dependent children, region, long-term illness and whether UK born.

[11] This is highly unlikely, given that all these factors are not available in Census data. For example, there are no controls for English language ability and time of arrival in the UK for immigrants. Unobserved differences in motivation, ability and so on are also likely to be included in the coefficients effect.

Figure C: Employment decomposition for male ethnic groups, 1991

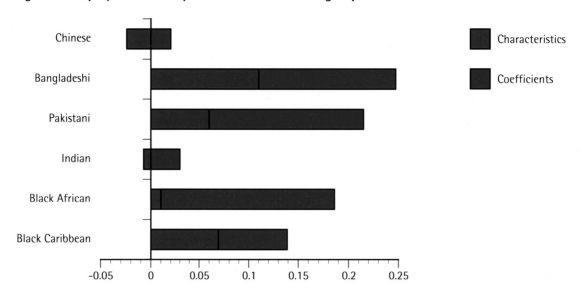

Source: 1991 SARs

In the figures, the further to the right that the bar extends indicates a larger employment advantage for the White group over the respective ethnic minority. Thus, Figure C confirms the findings of Table 1 that in 1991 there were large employment differentials between White men and their counterparts from each of the other groups, apart from Indians and the Chinese. Individuals from the latter group were actually very slightly more likely to be in employment. This is entirely due to this group possessing greater employment-enhancing characteristics relative to the White group since these characteristics were less well rewarded in comparison, as shown by the longer bar for the characteristics component lying to the left of the vertical axis and the shorter bar for the coefficients component lying to the right of the vertical axis. Indian men also possessed higher levels of employment-enhancing characteristics than White men but this was more than outweighed by the unexplained component, producing a 2.4 percentage point lower employment rate compared with White men. The difference in employment rates between Pakistani and Bangladeshi men and White men was more than 20 percentage points, a clear majority of which was left unexplained by characteristic differences. Men from the two Black groups also experienced far lower levels of employment than the White group. Again, very little of the differential between White and Black African men could be accounted for by characteristic differences, while for the Black Caribbean group around half of the differential could be explained.

Figure D shows that the relative position for men from each of the ethnic minorities had improved by 2001. However, the extent of these improvements varied. While the Black African, Pakistani and Bangladeshi groups experienced fairly large falls (in percentage point terms) in their employment differential relative to the White group, this was not the case for the Black Caribbean group. For the two most successful ethnic minorities, the small differential between the Indian and White groups that existed in 1991 had further narrowed, while the Chinese group extended its modest employment advantage over the White group between the two years. The improvement in the relative employment prospects of the Black African group can be attributed to the possession of better characteristics than the White group in 2001, while the characteristics component also fell for both the Pakistani and Bangladeshi groups.

Given the apparent importance of improvements in employment-enhancing characteristics, it is useful to ask which of the characteristics changed. Examination of the data reveals

Figure D: Employment decomposition for male ethnic groups, 2001

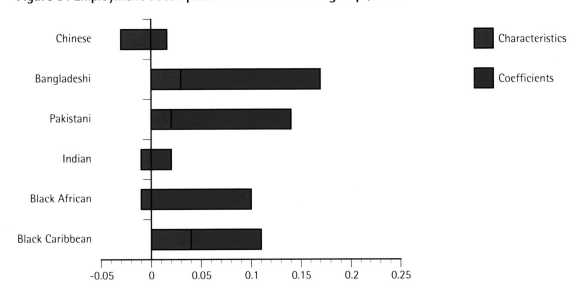

Source: 1991 SARs

that a 'better' age distribution in 2001 accounts for some of the improvement, especially for Bangladeshis. In other words, there were relatively more individuals in the prime age category for employment (aged 30-44) and relatively fewer in the age categories where employment rates are lower (especially younger men). A larger proportion of the Pakistani and Black African groups possessed higher qualifications than the White group in 2001. Leslie and Drinkwater (1999) identified a high proportion of ethnic minority individuals in higher and further education in 1991 and it is the movement of these cohorts into the labour market that helps to explain the improvement in the employment prospects of these groups and the relatively poorer performance of the Black Caribbean group, where educational participation is lower. Given that being foreign-born tends to reduce the employment probability, the decline in the percentage of immigrants among all ethnic minorities between 1991 and 2001, apart from Black Africans, also contributed to the reduction in the importance of the characteristics component.

It can be seen from Figures E and F that the position for women is somewhat different. First, Figure E shows that in 1991 the Black Caribbean group experienced a higher employment rate than the White group, despite having lower endowments of employment-enhancing characteristics. A potential explanation is that these women have higher proportions of single individuals and are thus under greater pressure to find employment as the sole earner in the household (Holdsworth and Dale, 1997). Second, the employment rate of White women was higher than that of all other groups in 1991, with the advantage over Pakistani and Bangladeshi women being particularly large. For both of these groups, the differential with the White group was more than 45 percentage points, less than half of which could be explained by endowments of characteristics. Factors such as religion, traditional gender roles, childcare and caring for older partners or relatives are likely to explain much of this difference. In contrast to men, Chinese women had lower levels of employment than White women, while the gap between Indian and White women was also greater than it was for men, with characteristics explaining most of the employment differences between these two groups and the White group in 1991.

Comparing Figures E and F reveals that there was less convergence for women between 1991 and 2001 in the employment rates of the White and ethnic minorities than was observed for men. The Black African and the South Asian groups did see some narrowing of the employment deficits with the White group but these reductions were small.

Figure E: Employment decomposition for female ethnic groups, 1991

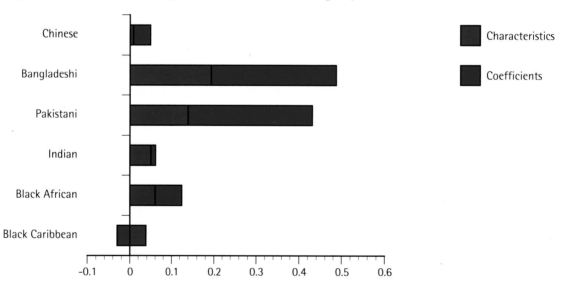

Source: 2001 CAMS

Figure F: Employment decomposition for female ethnic groups, 2001

Source: 2001 CAMS

Furthermore, unlike for men, this is not so much the outcome of rising endowments of employment-enhancing characteristics. For instance, while the explained component fell for each of the South Asian groups, it remains positive and fairly large in each case, with immigrant status and dependent children the most important factors. Furthermore, although the percentage of Pakistani and Bangladeshi women possessing higher qualifications increased between 1991 and 2001, it still lagged behind that of White women. The reduction in the contribution of the characteristics component for Indian women was due to this group having experienced a very large increase in the proportion with higher qualifications and also to a reduction in the proportion with dependent children.

The influence of three key factors on employment: 2001

Table 3 extends our understanding of the diversity of ethnic employment outcomes by showing the influence of three key variables on the probability of employment for each ethnic group in 2001. The table displays the marginal effects on the probability of employment of variables relating to religion, education and the general level of deprivation in the individual's neighbourhood. These variables are chosen since they have been found to be important influences on ethnic employment. Using the Fourth Survey of Ethnic Minorities, Brown (2000) and Lindley (2002) show how labour market outcomes vary with religion, while Clark and Drinkwater (2002), using the same dataset, demonstrate the influence of neighbourhood effects on employment. The 2001 Census offers an opportunity to investigate these variables further, since they appeared in the Census questionnaire for the first time in that year. Furthermore, the importance of education as a building block of employability is well known and the 2001 Census contained more detail on this than previous Censuses.[12] The marginal effects measure the impact of changing the relevant characteristic on the probability of employment for an individual from each ethnic group whose other characteristics are held at the average value for that group. Thus, the 0.018 entry for White British Christians at the top left of the table suggests that, compared with someone with no religion, the average White British Christian has a probability of employment that is 0.018 higher. Expressing probabilities of employment in percentage terms, this corresponds to a 1.8 percentage point increase.

Concerning religion, the table reports marginal effects for Christians and Muslims relative to those who stated that they had no religion.[13] The results suggest that Muslim men were less likely to be employed than those with no religion in 11 out of the 13 groups that had adequate sample sizes, although these differences were only statistically significant at the 10% level or lower for four of the groups: White British, Other White, Pakistani and Other. The large (16-20 percentage points) penalty faced by White Muslims is particularly notable. Bangladeshi Muslims had a (insignificantly) higher probability of employment than those with no religion, although 93% of Bangladeshis described themselves as Muslims. Pakistani Christians were significantly less likely to be employed but Christians accounted for only 1% of this ethnic group.

The table also shows that Muslim women had a lower employment rate for 12 out of the 13 groups, the exception being the Other Black group. The differences in employment rates between Muslims and those with no religion were in excess of 20 percentage points and significant at the 5% level for seven of the groups. The other religious effects were quite mixed for women: for example, Christians had significantly higher employment rates for White British, Other Black, Mixed: White & Black Caribbean and Other at the 10% level but significantly lower rates for Other White, Other Mixed and Indians.

As expected, the statistical models show that education had a positive, increasing and significant effect on employment for virtually all ethnic groups, with the largest impact for higher (level 4/5) qualifications. The marginal effect of possessing such qualifications relative to no formal qualifications is reported for all 16 ethnic groups, as shown in Table 3.[14] It can be seen that the marginal effects were generally higher for ethnic minorities than for the White British group. For example, the employment advantage of male Black African and Mixed: White & Black African higher education graduates over those with no qualifications was more than 30 percentage points, compared with less than

---

[12] Only selected marginal effects are reported in Table 3 for regression models estimated separately for each ethnic group. Table A2 in Appendix C contains estimates from pooled probit models for men and women, which include all of the explanatory variables.

[13] See Clark and Drinkwater (2005) for estimates that report the marginal effects for other religions.

[14] See Clark and Drinkwater (2005) for estimates of the effects of the full range of educational qualifications.

Table 3: Selected marginal effects for the probability of being in employment by ethnic group, England and Wales: 2001

	Male				Female			
	Christian	Muslim	Level 4/5 education	Index of Deprivation	Christian	Muslim	Level 4/5 education	Index of Deprivation
White British	0.018***	-0.159***	0.099***	-0.066***	0.029***	-0.203***	0.219***	-0.112***
White Irish	0.012	–	0.160***	-0.107***	-0.017	–	0.242***	-0.163***
Other White	0.009	-0.194***	0.142***	-0.163***	-0.040***	-0.275***	0.210***	-0.052*
Mixed: White & Black Caribbean	0.001	–	0.249***	-0.338***	0.115***	–	0.349***	-0.351***
Mixed: White & Black African	0.102	-0.138	0.342***	-0.141	0.056	-0.128	0.319***	-0.074
Mixed: White & Black Asian	0.038	-0.048	0.221***	-0.201**	0.016	-0.256***	0.265***	-0.321***
Other Mixed	-0.019	-0.081	0.214***	-0.161*	-0.088**	-0.248***	0.279***	-0.238**
Indian	-0.003	-0.032	0.150***	-0.072***	-0.097*	-0.307***	0.187***	-0.151***
Pakistani	-0.291***	-0.118*	0.218***	-0.351***	0.129	-0.008	0.325***	-0.455***
Bangladeshi	–	0.079	0.233***	-0.138**	–	-0.459***	0.454***	-0.389***
Other Asian	-0.024	-0.051	0.185***	-0.359***	0.015	-0.150*	0.349***	0.027
Black Caribbean	0.039*	-0.049	0.219***	-0.153***	0.037	-0.011	0.227***	-0.150***
Black African	0.023	-0.055	0.304***	-0.318***	-0.033	-0.248***	0.401***	-0.315***
Other Black	0.082	0.045	0.165***	-0.225***	0.150**	0.018	0.324***	-0.005
Chinese	-0.029	–	0.104***	0.027	0.019	–	0.164***	-0.070
Other	-0.081*	-0.289***	0.217***	-0.263***	0.180***	-0.030	0.169***	-0.048

Source: 2001 Census, CAMS. © Crown copyright

Notes: The regressions also controlled for age, marital status, children in household, region, health and whether UK born. All students are excluded from the analysis. Data relate to working-age population. For the religious effects, estimates are only reported if the cell size is at least 25. $*$ $p < 0.1$; $**$ $p < 0.05$; $***$ $p < 0.01$ (two-tailed tests).

10 percentage points for White British men. For women, the impact of human capital is again more important for most ethnic minorities compared with the White British group, especially for those with level 4/5 qualifications. For instance, Bangladeshi and Black African female graduates had an employment rate more than 40 percentage points higher than those with no qualifications, compared with an equivalent advantage of just over 20 percentage points for the White groups.

Table 3 also reports that the Index of Multiple Deprivation (IMD) had a negative and significant impact on employment probabilities at the 5% level for 13 of the 16 male groups,[15] the exceptions being the Other Mixed (significant at 10%), Mixed: White & Black African and Chinese groups, for whom employment rates were higher in more deprived areas. It can further be observed that women from the majority of the groups had significantly higher employment rates in less deprived areas, with the largest effects experienced by Pakistani and Bangladeshi women. In a sense, it is not surprising that for those in more deprived areas there are fewer employment opportunities. That there is ethnic diversity in the size of this effect is more interesting. While the White group also suffers lower employment rates in highly deprived areas, the marginal effects are generally larger for ethnic minorities. Given the disproportionate representation of ethnic minorities in relatively deprived, urban areas, the impact of the local area on employment, if not addressed by policy measures, has the potential to widen ethnic differences in labour market outcomes.

KEY POINTS

Census microdata from 1991 and 2001, together with more recent LFS data, demonstrate the considerable diversity and change in employment outcomes for ethnic minorities in England and Wales. Using employment rates excluding students, which we argue is the most appropriate measure, we find that, relative to the White group, there was an improvement for men from virtually all the ethnic minority groups, which can be consistently identified over time. This was particularly true for the Black African, Pakistani and Bangladeshi groups and can be explained in part by higher levels of human capital among these groups. Progress in employment rates relative to White men was much less for Black Caribbean men. For women there was also less of an increase in relative employment rates, while, for both men and women, some ethnic minorities continued to suffer serious disadvantage relative to the White group in 2001. Using data from the 2001 Census, we find that Muslims tend to have lower employment rates than those with no religion, although it is difficult to fully separate the effects of religion and ethnicity. We further find that employment is strongly positively correlated with education and negatively correlated with local deprivation. Furthermore, there are ethnic differences in these effects, which suggests that there may be some role for policy measures targeted at deprived areas and individuals that can alleviate ethnic employment disadvantage.

---

[15] This variable is measured on a continuous scale. See Appendix A for details of its construction.

3

Self-employment

Self-employment is widely thought to be an important form of economic activity for ethnic minorities in the UK. This broad generalisation, however, disguises considerable variation in self-employment rates by ethnicity and gender, and over space and time. In this chapter we provide a detailed picture of the dynamics and diversity of ethnic minority self-employment in Britain using Census microdata from 1991 and 2001.

Self-employment matters for ethnic minority welfare: working for oneself may be a positive choice to exploit particular talents or motivations and may be rewarding both financially and in terms of life or job satisfaction. On the other hand, working long hours to run a marginal business may be the only alternative to a labour market in which discrimination limits the opportunities available to certain groups. Previous research has emphasised these 'push' and 'pull' factors, which affect the choice between self-employment and paid employment. Metcalf et al (1996), for example, contrast the 'blocked upward mobility' approach to the understanding of Asian self-employment with the 'cultural resources' approach. Clark and Drinkwater (2000) find some evidence in favour of both push and pull factors: specifically, ethnic minority individuals respond to earnings differentials between paid and self-employment, thus paid labour market discrimination leads to higher self-employment for groups experiencing discrimination. At the same time, some aspects of ethnic minority culture such as religion may enhance entrepreneurial ambitions.

Previous research on self-employment in the UK has also found that:

- informal sources of finance are important for some ethnic minority businesses (Metcalf et al, 1996);
- there is little evidence that ethnic minority self-employment in Britain is the product of an enclave economy based around shared language, culture or the production of ethnic goods (Clark and Drinkwater, 2000, 2002);
- ethnic minority entrepreneurs earn substantially less than White entrepreneurs (Clark et al, 1998);
- ethnic minority entrepreneurs tend to be concentrated in industrial sectors with high business failure rates, such as retail, catering and transport (Parker, 2004);
- racial differences in access to start-up capital from banks exist (Parker, 2004);
- self-employment may enhance job satisfaction and feelings of self-worth, and may strengthen family ties (Metcalf et al, 1996);
- the employment of illegal immigrants by struggling ethnic minority businesses is common (Jones et al, 2006).

Figure G provides some context for the analysis conducted in the chapter. It presents aggregate statistics on self-employment rates for the UK. The self-employment rate is calculated here as the proportion of all those in either paid or self-employment who are self-employed. It is clear that the period we are examining has seen self-employment rates remain fairly stable, compared with the substantial growth of the 1980s. Growth in the 1980s has been attributed to a number of factors including changes in attitudes to entrepreneurship and business, the prevailing policy environment that encouraged business start-ups and the push from (long-term) unemployment (Weir, 2003). The increase in self-employment for ethnic minorities was particularly large: Daly (1991) reported that

Figure G: UK self-employment and unemployment rates, 1970–2004

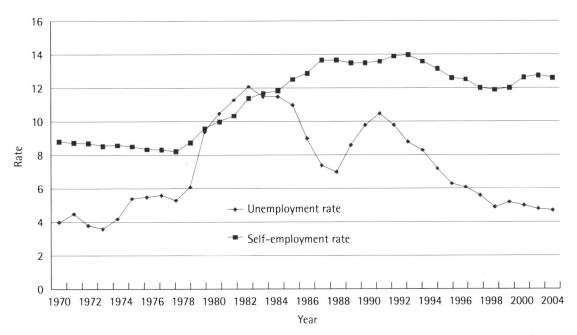

Source: Office for National Statistics

self-employment rates for ethnic minorities grew by 95% over the 1980s, compared with 52% for the White group.

By contrast, the 1990s saw a more favourable paid labour market than the previous decade, which may have accounted for the slow-down in the growth rate of entrepreneurship. Nevertheless, we will show that the generally stable pattern of self-employment in the aggregate data disguises considerable ethnic variation. We take a dynamic perspective and focus on how changes in the nature of the UK's ethnic minority population had an impact on self-employment over time. It is important to understand whether future generations of ethnic minorities will be as keen to enter self-employment as previous generations. If self-employment is declining, does this represent the closing down of a route to success for young ethnic minority individuals or indicate that they are no longer trapped in an 'economic dead end' (Aldrich et al, 1981)? We also exploit the detailed information in the 2001 Census to investigate how the characteristics of local areas affect the probability of self-employment.

A picture of ethnic minority self-employment

Table 4 presents self-employment rates calculated as the proportion of all those in paid and self-employment. For men, in both Census years there is considerable ethnic diversity in self-employment rates. In 1991 these varied from 9.1% for the Black Caribbean group to 34.1% for the Chinese. The two Black groups together with the Other category had lower rates than the White group, with the other 'Asian' groups having higher rates. Chinese and Pakistani men had relatively high proportions in self-employment, followed by the Indian, Bangladeshi and White groups. Moreover, the ranking of the groups stayed the same between 1991 and 2001; however, in contrast to the broadly steady aggregate self-employment rates shown in Figure G, there has been some important ethnic variation in the changes in self-employment rates over time. Broadly speaking, ethnic differences have narrowed: those groups with the highest self-employment rates – notably the Chinese and

Table 4: Self-employment rates by ethnic group

	1991			2001		
	Self-employment rate – all (%)	Self-employment rate – UK born (%)	N (all)	Self-employment rate – all (%)	Self-employment rate – UK born (%)	N (all)
Men						
White	16.6	16.5	247,074	17.0	16.9	398,278
Black Caribbean	9.1	7.1	1,975	13.0	10.6	3,470
Black African	12.2	9.4	608	13.5	11.7	2,869
Indian	23.7	15.2	3,777	21.4	13.1	8,002
Pakistani	26.6	15.3	1,364	26.5	18.1	4,073
Bangladeshi	18.8	15.2	431	19.1	11.2	1,433
Chinese	34.1	12.3	663	27.8	13.3	1,667
Other	13.4	12.7	2,321	16.2	12.8	6,645
All non-White	19.1		11,139	19.3		28,159
Women						
White	6.0	5.8	188,439	7.3	7.1	331,540
Black Caribbean	2.0	1.6	2,136	3.3	3.0	4,150
Black African	4.4	5.1	545	4.5	3.4	2,600
Indian	11.5	6.8	2,645	10.3	4.8	6,457
Pakistani	17.6	9.6	420	9.9	5.3	1,753
Bangladeshi	9.1	5.3	77	5.9	5.3	527
Chinese	20.3	9.5	558	18.3	9.2	1,533
Other	5.5	3.5	1,811	7.3	6.0	5,848
All non-White	8.1		8,192	8.0		22,868

Source: 1991 and 2001 Census, SARs. © Crown copyright

Indian groups – experienced a decline, while groups with initially low rates such as the Black Caribbean group showed some increase.

It is clear from the table that self-employment is much less important for women, with negligible proportions in this activity for most groups. The only exception is the Chinese group, where around 20% of workers were self-employed. While there is some evidence from other countries that female self-employment has been increasing, partly to allow female workers greater flexibility in childcare arrangements (Parker, 2004), there is little evidence of an increase in these data. This finding has been confirmed for the UK by Ajayi-Obe and Parker (2005). Indeed, Pakistani, Bangladeshi and Chinese women have seen a decline in their self-employment rate, substantially so for the former two groups. As shown in Figures A and B in Chapter 1, paid employment, on the other hand, has increased for women from all of the ethnic groups, with a corresponding shrinkage in the proportions of women counted as inactive.

Table 4 also provides self-employment rates, calculated separately for the UK born. Most immigrant members of the main ethnic groups in the UK arrived prior to the 1980s; hence, many of the people who now identify themselves as members of these groups are, in fact, second- or higher-generation immigrants. It is often argued that the high rates of self-employment seen among immigrant communities in many host economies reflect the greater entrepreneurial drive of immigrants. These are, it is claimed, individuals and families who are risk takers, prepared to seek out new opportunities in an unfamiliar environment. In fact, surveys of attitudes to risk do not always support this view (Metcalf et al, 1996; Bonin et al, 2006). However, it is likely that the native born will have a markedly different experience of socialisation and acquisition of formal and informal human capital to that of their parents. Hence, it is useful to examine the effect of being born in the UK.

From Table 4, it is clear that those born in the UK are less likely to be self-employed than first-generation immigrants, irrespective of ethnic group. This may be due to unobservable motivational factors that drive both the desire to migrate and the desire to start a business. On the other hand, some of this may reflect differences in age as, certainly for the ethnic minorities, the UK born will be younger on average. Nevertheless, some of the native–immigrant differences in Table 4 are substantial. For men from the Indian, Pakistani and Chinese groups, these are 10 percentage points or more. Similarly large differences are apparent for women from some of the groups. In subsequent sections we will examine the impact of being native born where age (and other factors) are controlled for.

Table 5 continues the theme of describing the nature of ethnic self-employment by presenting self-reported hours of work for the paid- and self-employed by gender, ethnicity and year. It is well established that the self-employed work longer hours than the paid-employed and this is confirmed in the Census data in both 1991 and 2001. For men, the size of the differential is positively correlated with a group's propensity for self-employment. Parker et al (2005) argue that the empirical regularity whereby the self-employed work longer hours but receive lower wages than the paid-employed is explained by the fact that the self-employed face greater income uncertainty. Longer hours compensate for the uncertainty by increasing the amount of income that the self-employed can 'guarantee', in other words, that is not affected by random shocks. Parker et al (2005) test this model using US data and find that self-employed workers with more uncertain incomes work longer hours. As noted by the Bank of England (1999), ethnic minorities in the UK tend to work in sectors where business failure rates are high; hence, this additional uncertainty might provide some explanation for the patterns we observe in the data. Blanchflower (2004) notes that, while job satisfaction as a whole is generally higher for the self-employed compared with the paid-employed, entrepreneurs in many countries of the world consistently report that they are less satisfied than paid employees with their hours of work.

Table 5: Hours of work for the paid- and self-employed by gender and ethnicity

| | Men | | | | Women | | | |
| | 1991 | | 2001 | | 1991 | | 2001 | |
	Paid	Self	Paid	Self	Paid	Self	Paid	Self
White	40.5	46.9	41.8	45.8	30.3	37.6	31.3	33.7
Black Caribbean	39.0	43.3	39.4	42.9	33.8	37.7	33.6	35.0
Black African	38.7	43.0	37.7	42.8	34.0	33.4	33.1	33.9
Indian	40.7	51.2	39.9	50.0	34.5	47.2	33.2	42.9
Pakistani	40.3	48.1	37.5	43.8	33.4	43.2	30.0	34.3
Bangladeshi	38.9	48.2	32.4	41.1	33.2	38.6	29.3	30.7
Chinese	41.4	49.6	38.9	48.4	34.8	46.8	33.8	43.1
Other	40.2	48.2	39.4	44.1	33.6	36.9	32.9	34.4

Source: 1991 and 2001 Census, SARs. © Crown copyright

Self-employment tends to be concentrated in particular types of industry. In a sense, this is not surprising: the start-up costs associated with many types of service sector activity are likely to always be much lower than those in manufacturing, for example. However, ethnic entrepreneurship is much more concentrated for some groups than for others. Figure H explores this idea by illustrating the industrial structure of self-employment for eight ethnic groups. There are some marked differences by ethnicity for both genders. For men, both White and Black Caribbean groups have relatively high proportions of the self-employed working in the construction sector (34% and 37% respectively in 1991). Black Africans and Indians have smaller proportions (5% and 8% respectively) in this sector, while the remaining groups have negligible numbers here. For the South Asian and Chinese groups, the combined category of distribution, hotels and catering accounts for a large proportion of the self-employed. Indeed, over 75% of male Chinese and Bangladeshi entrepreneurs worked in this sector in 1991. This sector includes both wholesale and retail trade as well as the operation of restaurants and other catering outlets. The transport sector was also a major source of self-employment for the Pakistani group in both Census years.

Over the period between Censuses, self-employment in transport grew for Pakistanis and Bangladeshis, with corresponding declines in distribution, hotels and catering. The White, Black Caribbean and Black African groups have seen a large increase in finance-based self-employment, with the increase (from 12% to 34%) particularly pronounced for the Black African group.

Women display a very different pattern of self-employment, with negligible proportions in construction or transport. Distribution, hotels and catering is again important, particularly for the Indian, Pakistani and Chinese groups. The residual, Other, category also accounts for a large proportion of self-employment for female entrepreneurs. Further investigation suggests that this is in the area of personal services and medical services. Non-negligible numbers of the female self-employed are also in finance. A large proportion of the Bangladeshi women self-employed in 1991 were in the manufacturing sector. However, an important caveat when discussing the results based on gender is that the number of female self-employed in our sample is very small; hence, these results should be treated with some caution.

Tables 6 and 7 further disaggregate the industry of the self-employed by reporting, only for men, a more detailed breakdown of the sector in which they work. This uses information on two-digit industries collected in each Census year. There are around 60 categories in total, and while these do not exactly match across Censuses, the breakdown allows a more detailed picture of the industry choice of ethnic minority entrepreneurs to be obtained. The tables report the five most important two-digit sectors for each group and the last row reports the proportion of all self-employment for each group accounted for by these five sectors. It is worth noting that even among White self-employed workers there is considerable concentration, with 65% of all entrepreneurs in the sample in the top five sectors. However, the other groups exhibit much greater concentration, rising in 1991 to over 90% of Chinese and Bangladeshi self-employment concentrated in the top five sectors. There is some evidence that this degree of concentration declined slightly between 1991 and 2001 but this was by no means a steep decline and around 80% of Bangladeshis and Chinese self-employed men were still concentrated in the top five sectors.

Figure H: Industrial distribution of self-employment by ethnicity

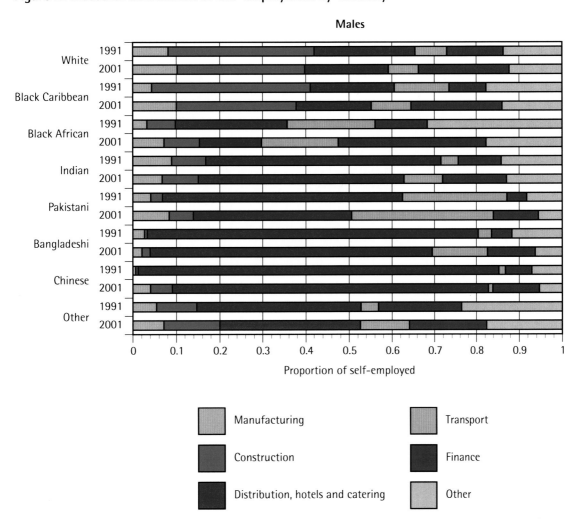

Males

Proportion of self-employed

Manufacturing   Transport

Construction   Finance

Distribution, hotels and catering   Other

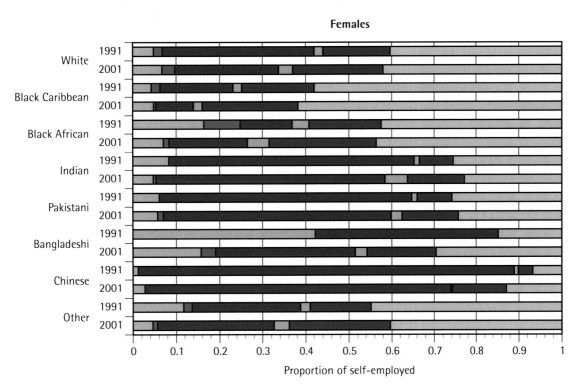

Females

Proportion of self-employed

Source: 1991 and 2001 SARs

Table 6: Detailed industry distribution of the self-employed, men 1991

Group	White	Black Caribbean	Black African	Indian	Pakistani	Bangladeshi	Chinese
2-digit industry	Construction	Construction	Other inland transport	Remainder of retail distribution	Remainder of retail distribution	Restaurants etc.	Restaurants etc.
	Business services	Other inland transport	Remainder distribution	Business services	Other inland transport	Medical and veterinary services	Business services
	Remainder of retail distribution	Business services	Business services	Construction	Restaurants etc.	Business services	Medical and veterinary services
	Agriculture	Remainder of retail distribution	Medical and veterinary services	Medical and veterinary services	Manufacture of leather, footwear, clothing	Manufacture of leather, footwear, clothing	Recreational and cultural services
	Other inland transport	Repair and servicing of motor vehicles	Recreational and cultural services	Manufacture of leather, footwear, clothing	Business services	Other inland transport	Wholesale distribution
5-industry concentration	65%	72%	63%	74%	81%	91%	92%

Source: 1991 Census, SARs. © Crown copyright

Table 7: Detailed industry distribution of the self-employed, men 2001

Group	White	Black Caribbean	Black African	Indian	Pakistani	Bangladeshi	Chinese
2-digit industry	Construction	Construction	Other business activities	Retail trade	Land transport	Hotels and restaurants	Hotels and restaurants
	Other business activities	Other business activities	Land transport	Health and social work	Retail trade	Land transport	Retail trade
	Agriculture	Retail trade	Construction	Construction	Hotels and restaurants	Retail trade	Other business activities
	Retail trade	Land transport	Computer and related activities	Other business activities	Wholesale trade	Other business activities	Construction
	Land transport	Computer and related activities	Retail trade	Wholesale trade	Construction	Wholesale trade	Health and social work
5-industry concentration	57%	56%	52%	62%	68%	78%	82%

Source: 2001 Census, CAMS. © Crown copyright

Decomposing the dynamics of ethnic entrepreneurship

In this section we examine the changing probabilities of self-employment for different ethnic groups using a decomposition procedure similar to that discussed in Chapter 2. Here, however, the differential to be decomposed involves differences in self-employment rates for the same ethnic group over time. Thus, we estimate what proportion of the change in the self-employment rate for, say, the White group between 1991 and 2001 is attributable to changes in the observed distribution of characteristics of the White group between these two years and what proportion is unexplained.

As before, this involves estimating separate regression models for each group in each year. Since self-employment accounts for a relatively small proportion of the labour force for some groups, particularly for women, we have collapsed the two Black groups and the Pakistani and Bangladeshi groups in this analysis. The separate regression models are not reported here. However, to provide some background for the subsequent analysis, Table A3 in Appendix C presents the marginal effects from a pooled regression model of the probability of being self-employed. The results suggest that, in line with previous research, self-employment increases with age but is lower for those with higher qualifications. The UK born are less likely to be self-employed compared with immigrants and home owners have higher self-employment rates, which may reflect greater access to capital. Controlling for these variables does not alter the broad rankings of the group's self-employment rates reported in Table 4.

The decomposition results are contained in Tables 8 and 9. The first row of the tables reports for each ethnic group the change in the self-employment rate between 1991 and 2001. The next two rows decompose this into the amount due to differences in observable characteristics between the two years and the amount due to changes in the estimated probit coefficients. For men (Table 8), as already shown in Table 4, three of the groups saw a decline in their self-employment rate over this period: Indians and the Chinese by 2.3 and 7.5 percentage points respectively,[16] while the Pakistani/Bangladeshi combined group saw a much smaller decline. For the Indians, the vast majority of this reduction in the self-employment rate is attributable to changes in observable characteristics, while for the Chinese the change is more evenly split between characteristics and coefficients (that is, unobservable factors), with characteristics responsible for over half the change. The Pakistani/Bangladeshi group is unusual here in that the decomposition suggests that the small reduction in self-employment rates is due to two offsetting sets of factors. Changes in the characteristics of the Pakistani/Bangladeshi group tended to reduce self-employment but this was almost entirely counteracted by a positive coefficients effect. Alternatively put, had only the characteristics of the Pakistani and Bangladeshi workers changed, their self-employment rate would have been almost 3 percentage points lower in 2001 compared with 1991.

Alone among the ethnic groups considered here, the Black group (which combines Black Africans and Black Caribbeans) saw a substantial increase in the self-employment probability. The majority of this was attributable to changes in coefficients; that is, it was not explainable by changes in observable characteristics.

The remainder of Table 8 breaks down the characteristics effect into its component parts for men. These are calculated using the method of Even and MacPherson (1993). Here, entries in the table reflect the proportion of the characteristics effect that is due to the relevant explanatory variable. Thus, for example, the 26% of the characteristics effect due to age for the Pakistani/Bangladeshi group implies that 26% of the reduction in the

---

[16] In fact, there are some slight discrepancies in these changes over time compared with Table 4. This is due to the regression sample being slightly different to that used to compute the descriptive statistics.

Table 8: Decomposition of the change in the self-employment probability by ethnic group for men

	White	Black	Indian	Pakistani/Bangladeshi	Chinese	Other
Differential $(P_{01} - P_{91}) \times 100$	0.30	3.34	-2.31	-0.17	-7.48	2.65
Coefficients	-0.36	2.73	-0.97	2.77	-3.45	3.10
Characteristics	0.66	0.69	-1.35	-2.94	-4.03	-0.45
% of characteristics due to:						
Age	61	122	13	26	13	5
Qualifications	-30	3	32	31	49	23
Marital status	-10	-1	38	6	34	71
Children	-9	7	8	7	8	21
UK born	1	-6	19	3	8	19
Illness	6	-1	-6	-1	1	-33
Housing tenure	71	-43	10	25	-7	-28
Region	11	19	-13	3	-7	21

Source: 1991 and 2001 Census, SARs. © Crown copyright

Note: Black refers to both Black Caribbean and Black African groups combined. The Pakistani and Bangladeshi groups have also been merged. Groups were merged to increase sample sizes as the decomposition procedure can be sensitive to missing cells in categorical variables.

self-employment probability attributable to characteristics is explained by the changing distribution of that variable over time. A negative entry in this part of the table would suggest that the explanatory variable in question was working in the opposite direction to the overall characteristics effect. Considering first the three Asian groups, which experienced declining self-employment rates, it is clear that age, education, marital status and country of birth were important influences on the characteristics effect and, hence, on the change in self-employment propensity over this period.

As noted earlier, an important development among ethnic minorities in the UK is that first-generation (that is, foreign-born) immigrants are being replaced in the workforce by the UK-born children of immigrants. In part this reflects changes in immigration policy, which have restricted immigration from British Commonwealth countries and in part the propensity of certain ethnic groups to have relatively large numbers of children. Thus, in our sample, the proportion of Pakistani and Bangladeshi men who were aged under 30 in 1991 was 35%. By 2001 this had risen to 40%. For Indians the corresponding percentages were 27% in 1991 and 29% in 2001. Although these are not huge increases in percentage-point terms, the strong positive influence of age on self-employment probabilities makes this shift in the age distribution of ethnic minorities a contributory factor to the reductions in entrepreneurship for these groups.

In a similar vein, increasing educational attainment has been a feature of the experience of young members of these ethnic minorities in the UK: over the period in question the proportion of Indians in our sample with a higher qualification grew from 24% to 41%. The equivalent figures for the Pakistani/Bangladeshi and Chinese groups are from 14% and 33% to 27% and 43% respectively. The importance for self-employment rates is clear from the regression models: higher qualifications are associated with paid employment rather than self-employment and the increasing educational attainment of these groups has contributed to a reduction in self-employment.

In 2001, members of the Indian and Chinese groups were less likely to be married and more likely to be single than in 1991. Given the association between marital status and self-employment, this contributed to the reduction in self-employment. Similarly, the proportions of the three Asian groups who were born in the UK rose from 14% to 31% for Indians, from 13% to 26% for Pakistanis and Bangladeshis and from 9% to 19% for the Chinese. The regression models show that immigrants are more likely to be self-employed than the UK born and again this contributed to reductions in self-employment propensity.

For these three groups the results suggest that, relative to their parents, second-generation immigrants find self-employment a less attractive form of activity than the paid labour market. To some extent, this may reflect the age and stage in the life cycle of the second generation: as they get older and settle down, entrepreneurship may again grow. However, it is interesting to note that, for the Indian and Chinese groups, the decompositions pick out qualifications and immigrant status, more than age per se as the key influences driving the characteristics effect. For the Pakistani/Bangladeshi group, age itself is an important factor and for this group the positive coefficients effect suggests that there exist positive influences on self-employment that are not being captured by observable characteristics. Any discussion of what these factors might be is necessarily speculative; nonetheless, there is evidence that this group is likely to face more discrimination in the paid labour market and also that these predominantly Muslim individuals may prefer to live away from the majority white community or from other groups (Blackaby et al, 1999), which may lead to working for themselves rather than doing paid work.

Like the Pakistani and Bangladeshi groups, the Black group exhibits a positive coefficients effect and this is the major component of an increasing self-employment rate between the two Census years. Again this may reflect paid employment discrimination or more positive pull factors leading Black workers to set up in business for themselves.

Table 9 reports the results of conducting a similar exercise for women. It should be noted here that the smaller samples of economically active women and relatively low female self-employment rates suggest that these results should be treated with more caution than

Table 9: Decomposition of the change in the self-employment probability by ethnic group for women

	White	Black	Indian	Pakistani/Bangladeshi	Chinese	Other
Differential $(P_{01} - P_{91}) \times 100$	1.31	1.28	−1.16	−7.33	−2.43	1.94
Coefficients	0.74	1.04	−0.93	−5.17	0.50	1.75
Characteristics	0.57	0.23	−0.23	−2.16	−2.93	0.19
% of characteristics due to:						
Age	45	71	−28	12	12	70
Qualifications	4	36	−78	11	55	92
Marital status	−13	−4	105	8	33	−60
Children	7	1	44	1	9	−23
UK born	2	−6	123	31	5	−16
Illness	7	7	−33	0	−4	38
Housing tenure	43	−11	−42	22	−13	64
Region	5	7	9	16	1	−65

Source: 1991 and 2001 Census, SARs. © Crown copyright
Note: See note to Table 8.

those for men. Two groups stand out: the Pakistani/Bangladeshi group experienced a large decline in the self-employment rate over the period, most of which was not attributable to observable characteristics. On the other hand, characteristics changes were responsible for the declining Chinese female rate. In fact, for Chinese women, qualifications, marital status and country of birth acted in much the same way as for their male counterparts.

Enclaves, neighbourhood effects and self-employment

As we have seen in the previous chapter, the impact of neighbourhood characteristics on economic activity is potentially important. In the case of self-employment, this has been viewed as a particularly interesting source of variation. A considerable amount of previous work has investigated the idea that high rates of self-employment among minority and immigrant communities reflect an 'enclave' economy whereby self-sustaining communities develop based around shared ethnicity, culture, language or religion. Such communities offer additional sources of product demand for ethnic-specific goods and services, may imply lower levels of consumer discrimination against ethnic minorities, and can provide easy access to networks of information, credit, potential workers and other business services (see Parker, 2004, pp 120-1). If this is the case, we would expect to find the percentage of an individual's own group in their local area to have a positive influence on that individual's self-employment probability. The existing literature, based on datasets from various countries, presents conflicting evidence on the impact of geographical concentrations of ethnic minorities on self-employment rates. For the UK, the available evidence, based on different, complementary datasets suggests that for ethnic minorities in the UK there is a negative effect of co-ethnic concentration on self-employment rates, even when controlling for other observable characteristics. These results have led to the conclusion that the relatively deprived nature of ethnically concentrated areas in Britain serves to depress self-employment opportunities rather than to foster an enclave economy (Clark and Drinkwater, 1998, 2000, 2002). In this section we update this work using 2001 Census microdata and explore the effect of alternative measures of neighbourhood characteristics on self-employment rates.

Table 10 illustrates the results of adding variables reflecting features of the local area to ethnic-specific regression models of self-employment propensity. For 1991, areas are defined as the so-called 'Samples of Anonymised Records (SARs) areas'. These are mainly local authority areas, with some areas created by amalgamating adjacent local authorities, and there were around 278 of them in 1991, with a minimum population size of 120,000. In 2001 we use local/unitary authorities, data from which were merged into the 2001 individual SARs dataset. There were 409 such areas with an average population of around 140,000. Note that as well as collapsing the ethnic groups as we did in the last section, we also combine men and women in these analyses.

In each panel of Table 10 there are four rows. The first reports the marginal effect of the local unemployment rate on the probability of self-employment. This marginal effect comes from an ethnic-specific regression model where in addition to the variables used in the previous regression models, the local unemployment rate has been added as an additional explanatory variable. In the second row the same thing is done for the percentage of the local population that is of the same ethnic group as the individual. Thus in the White group regression this is the percentage White and so on. In the third and fourth rows of the table both of these variables are added together to the regression model to investigate the impact of one local area effect, controlling for the other. The interpretation of the marginal effects is as follows. Consider the −0.003 effect for the White group in the first row of Table 10(a). This means that, controlling for individual characteristics, an increase in the local unemployment rate by 1 percentage point from its average value (e.g from 10%

Table 10: Local area effects on self–employment by ethnic group

	White	Black	Indian	Pakistani/Bangladeshi	Chinese
(a) 1991					
Unemployment rate	-0.003***	-0.001	-0.001	0.002	0.002
Percentage own group	0.001***	-0.003***	-0.004***	-0.011***	-0.138**
Unemployment rate	-0.003***	-0.000	0.003	0.007**	0.005
Percentage own group	0.001***	-0.003***	-0.005***	-0.014***	-0.168**
N	429,403	5,114	6,348	2,271	1,175
(b) 2001					
Unemployment rate	-0.006***	-0.002	-0.008***	-0.010***	-0.011**
Percentage own group	0.001***	-0.001*	-0.004***	-0.003***	-0.081**
Unemployment rate	-0.005***	-0.001	-0.002	0.004	-0.008**
Percentage own group	0.000**	-0.001	-0.004***	-0.011***	-0.068**
N	621,027	9,289	12,651	6,697	2,336

Source: 1991 Census SARs and 2001 Census CAMS. © Crown copyright

Notes: The full regression model also contained controls for age, education, marital status, gender, illness, housing tenure, region, marital status, whether UK born children in household. * indicates statistical significance at 10%, ** at 5% and *** at 1%.

to 11%) leads to a 0.3 percentage point decline in the self-employment probability of White workers.

Considering 1991 first, previous conclusions about the impact of ethnic concentration on self-employment are confirmed, with negative effects on self-employment for all groups except the White group. These are also statistically significant in most cases. The magnitude of these effects may seem quite small in percentage-point terms but one should consider the range of variation of the underlying variable. For example, while the typical Indian in 1991 lived in an area where around 7.7% of the population was of the same ethnic origin, this percentage ranged from 0.02% to 22.3%. Moving from an area with the lowest proportion of Indians (for example, Banff and Buchan) to one with the highest (Leicester) would imply a reduction in the Indian self-employment rate of around 6.5 percentage points. The large size of the Chinese marginal effect is also worth noting – this is statistically significant in the model where both local area variables are included together. This reflects the extremely dispersed nature of Chinese settlement in the UK. The Chinese are the least likely to live in areas with a high concentration of co-ethnics. In 1991, using these data, the typical Chinese individual lived in an area where Chinese comprised 0.5% of the population. Furthermore, this ranged from 0.06% to 1.6%.

Unemployment rates were negative and statistically significant only for the White group in 1991. Interestingly, they were positive for Pakistanis and Bangladeshis and the Chinese, but only statistically significant for the former. This may reflect workers being pushed into self-employment due to poor local labour market conditions for this group.

Turning to 2001, the unemployment rate in the models where it enters on its own is uniformly negative, and significant for all of the ethnic groups except the Black group. The effect is most pronounced for the Pakistani/Bangladeshi group. The percentage own group variable is again negative and significant for all groups except the White group. Including both variables in the model makes the unemployment variable insignificant in all cases except for the White and Chinese groups. Unemployment rates and percentage own group are positively correlated for all ethnic minorities in the data but negatively correlated for the White group.

One caveat to the above analysis is that the areas that we investigate are too big to be properly classed as neighbourhoods and the kinds of enclave and neighbourhood effects that we are investigating may take place at a lower level of geography. Unfortunately, with the data available to us, we are not able to identify which local authority ward individuals reside in; however, we can use the Index of Multiple Deprivation (IMD), which is collected at a lower level of aggregation.

Figure I illustrates the results of introducing the IMD score into a regression model like that reported in Table A3 in Appendix C. The coefficient on the IMD is negative for all the groups and significantly so for the White, Indian and the (combined) Pakistani/Bangladeshi groups; however, the figure gives some idea of the magnitude of the estimated effect. Clearly, it is the Pakistani/Bangladeshi group where self-employment declines the most with local deprivation. From very low levels of deprivation to levels of around 60 corresponds to a reduction in the self-employment rate of around 8 percentage points for this group and around 4 percentage points for the Indians. To give some idea of what these levels of deprivation mean, the three lowest-ranked local authority areas were Hart, Wokingham and Surrey Heath. These had IMD scores of around 1, while scores of around 60 corresponded to the average value in local authority areas such as Liverpool, Knowsley and Tower Hamlets.

Figure I: Multiple deprivation and self-employment by ethnic group

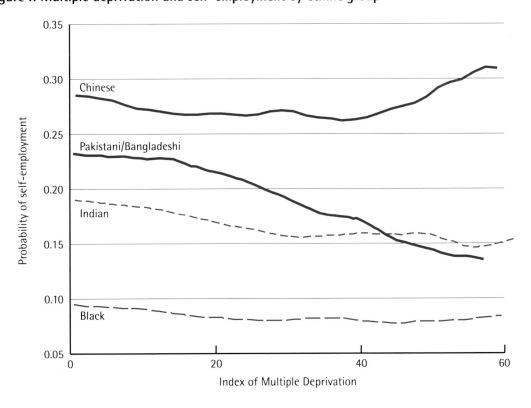

Source: 2001 CAMS
Note: The figure reports the predicted rate of self-employment for a 'typical' individual from each ethnic group. These are based on a partially linear model (Robinson, 1988; Yatchew, 2003) that controlled for age, marital status, housing tenure, illness, education and region.

KEY POINTS

In this chapter we have argued that it is useful to consider self-employment when discussing the welfare of ethnic minorities in the UK. Among men, there is considerable ethnic diversity in self-employment rates: Asian groups tend to favour this form of activity while Black groups do not. With the exception of the Chinese, women do not tend to be self-employed. Male self-employment is concentrated in a few key sectors – in particular transport and catering – and the self-employed work longer hours than employees. Over the period 1991-2001 there has been some convergence in self-employment rates between ethnic minorities. Part of this convergence is explained by changes in the composition of ethnic minorities – younger, better-educated, UK-born individuals are less likely to be self-employed than their parents. There is little evidence that self-employment is an 'enclave' phenomenon but for some groups their geographical concentration in relatively deprived areas reduces entrepreneurial opportunities.

Occupation and earnings

The previous chapters have examined the factors influencing how people find work and whether they choose paid or self-employment. Clearly finding a job is not the end of the story and experiences in work can potentially vary with gender and ethnicity. In this chapter, we focus on how the success of those who are in paid work differs by ethnic group and examine how these achievements have evolved in recent times. To do this, we use two different data sources. We begin by examining how social class outcomes have changed for the main ethnic groups between 1991 and 2001 using Census microdata. Second, since no questions on earnings are asked in the Census, we analyse recent information from the Labour Force Survey (LFS) to establish how pay varies by ethnic group, both in general terms and within broad occupations.

Changes in occupational attainment during the 1990s are likely to have been affected by the changing structure of the UK labour market. Of particular relevance here is the impact of technological change on the labour market. The influence of skill-biased technological change, whereby recent technological advances have been biased in favour of skilled workers and against unskilled workers, may be important here. It has been argued that technological change has brought about an increase in the demand for skilled workers and a worsening of job prospects for those who are less skilled. To the extent that skills are unequally distributed across ethnic groups, skill-biased technological change may impact on the relative occupational attainment and earnings of those groups.

More recent contributions, such as the influential paper by Autor et al (2003), also need to be considered within this framework. Autor et al (2003) have amended some of the predictions of the skill-biased technological change literature by suggesting that there has also been an increase in demand for some low-skilled jobs because technology has been unable to replace some non-routine functions. The types of manual non-routine jobs they refer to include janitorial services and lorry driving, since there are limited opportunities for the substitution of these activities by information technologies. Goos and Manning (2003) provide empirical support for this hypothesis using UK data.

Another important development in literature on the labour market over this period is the idea of 'overeducation'. It is argued here that the rapid increase in educational attainment over time, particularly at the graduate level, has led to some workers with high levels of education being overqualified for the jobs in which they are employed. Evidence in support of this argument has been found by numerous studies. For example, Green and McIntosh (2006: forthcoming), using the Skills Survey, report that the percentage who were overqualified for the jobs that they were doing rose from 32% to 37% between 1997 and 2001, while over the same period, the percentage who were underqualified remained roughly the same at around 20%. Given the increase in educational participation of many ethnic minorities noted by Drew (1995) and Leslie and Drinkwater (1999), how recent graduates from the ethnic communities have fared in the job market is an important issue that will be the focus of this chapter. Battu and Sloane (2004) argue that ethnic minorities are more likely to be overeducated than the White group in the UK – it follows that employment rates might not give a complete indication of the welfare of particular groups if those groups are doing jobs for which they are overeducated.

There have been previous attempts to track changes in occupational attainment by ethnic group in the UK over time. For example, Heath and Yu (2005) examine the evolution of ethnic penalties using data from the General Household Survey (GHS) and LFS. For men, they find that first-generation Black, Indian and Pakistani migrants (born 1940-59 and interviewed in the 1970s) faced significant ethnic penalties in terms of access to professional/managerial jobs (which they term the salariat). They argue that earlier cohorts were disadvantaged in terms of their human capital, especially their lack of UK-attained educational qualifications and language skills. Since then, while subsequent generations have invested heavily in increasing their skills, direct labour market discrimination still exists.

Platt (2005a, 2005b) considers the intergenerational social mobility of ethnic minorities over time by examining the Office for National Statistics Longitudinal Study. Platt (2005a) argues that ethnic minorities started from a very different occupational structure in 1971, with this and patterns of migration shaping the achievements of the groups in 1991. In particular, she finds that, of those with higher occupational attainment in the first generation, Indians were able to maintain these achievements in the next generation. In contrast, the relative occupational position of Caribbeans had slipped by 1991. She also reports that the occupational position of women from the ethnic minority communities was more dependent on their origins than it was for men. Platt (2005b) adds data from the 2001 Census to further investigate the evolution of occupational achievement for ethnic minorities. It is found that Caribbeans, Black Africans, Indians, Chinese and Others experienced upward occupational mobility relative to the White UK born, after origins had been taken into account. However, the Pakistani and Bangladeshi groups performed less well in terms of occupational achievement. By examining the information on religion from the 2001 Census, it is reported that some diversity exists within groups: for the Indian group, Hindus outperformed Sikhs and Muslims.

Modelling success at the workplace

Many authors have used binary statistical models to examine occupational differences by ethnic group. For example, Heath and McMahon (1997) estimate a series of logistic models for first- and second-generation ethnic minority men and women using the 1991 SARs, based on the Goldthorpe Class categorisation.[17] Ethnic penalties are measured via the inclusion of a set of ethnic minority dummy variables in a pooled regression model. Their main finding was that the occupational attainment of ethnic minorities was very similar across the two generations. Heath et al (2000) also reach a similar conclusion by estimating logistic regressions to examine ethnic penalties in terms of the probability of just being in the salariat using the 1991 Samples of Anonymised Records (SARs) and the LFS.

Rather than estimating models using a binary dependent variable, some studies analyse occupational attainment by applying models that have a categorical dependent variable. For example, Carmichael and Woods (2000) estimate an ordered probit model using the LFS based on social class data. Since they do not find that differences relative to the White group cannot be fully explained by human capital and personal characteristics for Black, Indian and Pakistani/Bangladeshi men and women, they argue that some discrimination exists on the part of employers. Borooah (2001) uses a multinomial logit to model occupational success among White, Black Caribbean and Indian men. The three categories of the dependent variable are unskilled, skilled and professional/managerial (and technical). The decomposition results suggest that the occupational disadvantage

---

[17] The three sets of logistic regressions that are estimated are Goldthorpe Classes 1 and 2 versus Classes 3-7, Class 4 versus 3 and 5-7 and Classes 3, 5 and 6 versus Class 7.

suffered by Black Caribbeans was as much due to their characteristics as their ethnicity but the superior attributes of Indians were outweighed by an ethnic occupational penalty.

In our analysis, we estimate binomial probit models for the probability of being in the managerial/professional and unskilled/partly skilled social classes. The social classes are combined in this way because of the need to achieve adequate cell sizes for each of the ethnic groups. We focus on both the upper and lower ends of the occupational spectrum because of the observed polarisation of jobs in the UK noted by Goos and Manning (2003). The advantage of estimating binomial probit models is that marginal effects can easily be computed and interpreted, especially relative to multinomial models where they need to be compared with a particular base category. Furthermore, it has also been found that multinomial models provide virtually no advantage over binomial models (Alvarez and Nagler, 1998).

However, given that occupation is not a continuous variable, the use of categorical or dichotomous models to estimate success at work has been criticised. Therefore, in the context of UK ethnic minorities, Modell (1999) analyses a range of continuous measures of occupational attainment (for example, Goldthorpe Class, SIOPS, ISEI, CAMSCORE and NESSCORE). She finds that native-born ethnic minorities have better occupational outcomes and that Indian men outperform their Black Caribbean counterparts, whereas the opposite is true for women. Stewart (1983) also criticises studies that use categorical measures of occupational attainment. Instead, he matches occupational earnings from the GHS to occupational categories in the National Training Survey as he argues that this makes it abundantly clear what is being measured. This approach also provides the advantage of being able to examine the relative importance of within-occupational earnings differences. Therefore, in addition to estimating measures of success at work based on discrete dependent variables, we also estimate wage equations based on a continuous measure of earnings. Analysis of earnings is also more popular in the economics literature, as opposed to the sociological literature, where occupational studies have tended to dominate.

Ethnic differences in occupational attainment, 1991–2001

Given the changes to occupational classifications between 1991 and 2001, there is a need to be able to compare occupational attainment on a consistent basis across these two years. In order to do this, we make use of ONS (2005), which has suggested consistent definitions for both social class and socioeconomic group based on the National Statistics Socio-economic Classification (NS-SEC) variable for 2001. Information on social class outcomes for the main ethnic groups in Britain for men and women can be found in Tables A4 and A5 in Appendix C. We examine social class rather than socioeconomic group because some cell sizes are very small for some groups.

In order to examine changes over time in more detail, we refer to Figures J and K, which report percentage-point differences in six consistently defined social classes between 1991 and 2001. It can be seen from J that the percentage with managerial jobs rose for all ethnic groups, with the largest increases for men achieved by Black Caribbeans, Black Africans and Indians. Figure K reveals that for women, Indians experienced the highest increase in the percentage in managerial occupations. The percentage in professional occupations also increased for women in all eight ethnic groups, whereas only Black Caribbean men saw a rise in the percentage in this category between 1991 and 2001. The increase in those with higher-level occupations therefore appears consistent with the literature on skill-biased technological change.

Figure J: Percentage-point change in social class distribution for male ethnic groups, 1991–2001

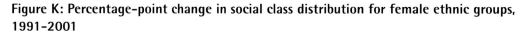

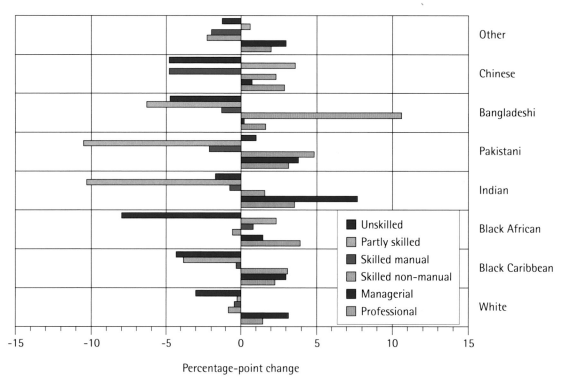

Source: 1991 and 2001 SARs

Figure K: Percentage-point change in social class distribution for female ethnic groups, 1991–2001

Source: 1991 and 2001 SARs

There was a general decrease in the proportion in intermediate occupations such as skilled manual workers, which appears to support the arguments of Autor et al (2003) and Goos and Manning (2003). Chinese and Bangladeshi men saw particularly large decreases in the percentage with skilled manual jobs between 1991 and 2001, as was the case for Pakistani and Indian women. However, seven out of the eight ethnic groups experienced a fall in the percentage in unskilled occupations, for both men and women. Therefore, the suggestions of Autor et al (2003) and Goos and Manning (2003) that there has been an increase in demand for some manual occupations do not appear to be borne out by the SARs data split by ethnic group. The reason for this discrepancy could be because the social class categories used in this analysis, which are needed to analyse ethnic groups separately, are too broad to pick up those low-skilled occupations where employment may have risen. Alternatively, most of the increases in these occupations could have occurred before the 1990s, given that Goos and Manning's study covers the period from around 1976 to 1999. However, an exception to the general trend in the SARs data is White men, since the proportion in unskilled jobs did actually increase by more than 1 percentage point between 1991 and 2001, and, given that the White group makes up the vast majority of the workplace, this may still be in line with the findings of Goos and Manning (2003).

Marginal effects from the probit models estimating the probability of being in professional/ managerial or partly skilled/unskilled occupations are reported in Tables 11 and 12. Despite the increases in educational attainment for many ethnic minorities over the 1990s, it can be seen from Table 11 that there were only relatively small differences for men from the ethnic minorities in 1991 and 2001. This contrasts with the results from Figure J and suggests that changes in the observable characteristics of the different groups explained much of the apparent increase in occupational attainment over this period. The only group to experience substantial advancement in their relative occupational attainment was the Black Caribbean group, whose disadvantage relative to the White group in terms of professional/managerial occupations fell from 16 to 8 percentage points. A similar picture emerges for women in Table 12, since the differentials between the White group and each ethnic minority in terms of being in a professional/managerial occupation remained virtually identical in 2001 compared with 1991. One exception is Bangladeshi women, whose position did worsen, although the 1991 results are based on quite a small sample for this group.

For most of the groups, between 1991 and 2001, there was also an increase in the probability of being in a partly skilled or unskilled occupation compared with the White

Table 11: Marginal effects for social class outcomes for men by ethnic group, 1991 and 2001

	Professional/managerial		Partly skilled/unskilled	
	1991	2001	1991	2001
Black Caribbean	-0.163***	-0.083***	0.058***	0.023***
Black African	-0.177***	-0.187***	0.129***	0.132***
Indian	-0.107***	-0.078***	0.069***	0.051***
Pakistani	-0.152***	-0.166***	0.108***	0.136***
Bangladeshi	-0.242***	-0.219***	0.179***	0.247***
Chinese	-0.060**	-0.063***	-0.041**	0.139***
Other	-0.011	-0.052***	-0.006	0.040***

Source: 1991 and 2001 Census, SARs. © Crown copyright

Notes: Controls included for higher education, age, marital status, whether UK born and region. Data relate to working-age population. ** $p < 0.05$; *** $p < 0.01$ (two-tailed tests).

Table 12: Marginal effects for social class outcomes for women by ethnic group, 1991 and 2001

	Professional/managerial		Partly skilled/unskilled	
	1991	2001	1991	2001
Black Caribbean	0.016	−0.013	0.012	−0.007
Black African	−0.106***	−0.111***	0.123***	0.115***
Indian	−0.114***	−0.102***	0.087***	0.045***
Pakistani	−0.068***	−0.083***	0.088***	0.042***
Bangladeshi	−0.005	−0.077***	0.082	0.005
Chinese	−0.068***	−0.063***	0.003	0.040***
Other	−0.034***	−0.038***	0.008	0.037***

Source: 1991 and 2001 Census, SARs. © Crown copyright

Notes: Controls included for higher education, age, marital status, whether UK born and region. Data relate to working-age population. *** $p < 0.01$ (two-tailed tests).

group. Again the main group to experience an improvement in occupational status at the bottom end of the occupational scale was the Black Caribbean group, while the position of the Pakistani and Bangladeshi groups worsened over the 1990s. Chinese men actually went from being less likely to have unskilled or partly skilled jobs to having a probability of around 14 percentage points higher than White men in 2001. However, there was a general improvement for women from the ethnic minority communities, since the higher incidence of being in a partly skilled or unskilled occupation was reduced for five out of the seven ethnic minorities between 1991 and 2001.

Key determinants of occupational achievement

Given the similar conclusions reached by Heath and McMahon (1997) and Heath et al (2000), the subsequent statistical analysis of occupational outcomes focuses solely on the probability of having a professional/managerial job. Tables 13 and 14 contain marginal effects on some of the main influences that affect the probability of having a professional or managerial job, separately by ethnic group. These factors are living in London or the South East, having higher qualifications and being native born. Such groupings were chosen because of the need to achieve reasonable cell sizes, since the sample sizes for some ethnic groups were quite small.

Several consistent findings can be identified across ethnic groups in terms of the impact of key influences. Being a higher education graduate increased the probability of having a professional/managerial job by between 49 and 73 percentage points for men and between 55 and 67 percentage points for women in 1991. The impact of having a higher qualification fell quite considerably for each ethnic group between 1991 and 2001, except for Chinese men. For most groups the impact of being a higher education graduate was around 10 percentage points smaller in 2001 but for some ethnic groups the reduction was even greater. For example, the advantage of Bangladeshi men with a higher qualification fell by almost 30 percentage points and by over 16 percentage points for Black African and Indian women.

To further examine the impact of the increasing proportion of higher education graduates among some ethnic groups, Tables 13 and 14 also report the marginal effects for a term that interacts the higher education and 2001 dummies on pooled data for 1991 and 2001.

Table 13: Marginal effects on the probability of being in the professional/managerial social class for men by ethnic group, 1991 and 2001

	White		Black Caribbean		Black African		Indian		Pakistani		Bangladeshi		Chinese		Other	
	1991	2001	1991	2001	1991	2001	1991	2001	1991	2001	1991	2001	1991	2001	1991	2001
Higher qualifications	0.601***	0.507***	0.575***	0.473***	0.491***	0.404***	0.626***	0.536***	0.597***	0.485***	0.728***	0.441***	0.545***	0.618***	0.548***	0.522***
London/South East	0.107***	0.093***	0.020	0.016	-0.157***	-0.151***	0.114***	0.045***	0.082***	0.103***	0.057*	0.026	0.087	0.054	0.029	0.021
UK born	-0.029***	-0.019***	0.026	0.068	-0.022	0.088	-0.013	0.015	0.115***	0.121***	-0.005	0.103**	0.226***	0.074	0.002	0.056***
N	201,023	320,191	1,735	2,893	502	2,184	2,826	5,880	982	2,765	337	1,059	427	1,071	1,874	5,112
Higher*2001	-0.081***		-0.043		-0.046		-0.087***		-0.100***		-0.121***		-0.010		-0.102***	
N	521,214		4,628		2,686		8,706		3,747		1,396		1,498		6,986	

Source: 1991 and 2001 Census, SARs. © Crown copyright

Notes: Controls are also included for age and marital status. Data relate to the working-age population. * $p < 0.1$; ** $p < 0.05$; *** $p < 0.01$ (two-tailed tests).

Table 14: Marginal effects on the probability of being in the professional/managerial social class for women by ethnic group, 1991 and 2001

	White		Black Caribbean		Black African		Indian		Pakistani		Bangladeshi		Chinese		Other	
	1991	2001	1991	2001	1991	2001	1991	2001	1991	2001	1991	2001	1991	2001	1991	2001
Higher qualifications	0.671***	0.567***	0.623***	0.493***	0.638***	0.468***	0.654***	0.492***	0.551***	0.445***	0.561***	0.445***	0.665***	0.578***	0.611***	0.485***
London/South East	0.045***	0.041***	-0.037	-0.014	-0.153*	-0.153***	0.063***	0.006	0.016	-0.034	-0.024	0.014	0.085	0.060*	-0.029	-0.026*
UK born	-0.021***	0.008*	-0.044	0.005	-0.100*	0.031	0.005	0.078***	0.001	0.067**	0.225	0.122**	0.042	-0.061	0.004	0.058***
N	176,034	293,369	2,043	3,802	499	2,161	2,299	5,355	340	1,417	65	425	440	1,107	1,671	4,923
Higher*2001	-0.108***		-0.172***		-0.158***		-0.141***		-0.107***		-0.114		-0.132***		-0.141***	
N	469,403		5,845		2,660		7,654		1,757		490		1,547		6,594	

Source: 1991 and 2001 Census, SARs. © Crown copyright

Notes: Controls are also included for age and marital status. Data relate to the working-age population. * $p < 0.1$; ** $p < 0.05$; *** $p < 0.01$ (two-tailed tests).

For men, the largest marginal effects were seen for Bangladeshis, followed by Others, Pakistanis and Indians. Educational changes had the smallest impact for the two Black groups and the Chinese. The negative interaction terms tended to be larger for women, since they were at least 10 percentage points for each ethnic group and were particularly large for Black Caribbeans, Black Africans, Others and Indians. This tends to suggest that the positive impact of education on occupational attainment was lower in 2001 compared with 1991. This is consistent with the idea that an excess supply of (minority) graduates has reduced the returns from education.

Having been born in the UK also tends to exert a positive influence on the probability of having a professional/managerial occupation but the impact of this variable is not generally that strong. For example, the only groups where the advantage of the UK born was greater than 10 percentage points in 2001 were Pakistani and Bangladeshi men and Bangladeshi women. There was an increase in the occupational advantage of the UK born for those from Other ethnic groups, while for the Chinese, this advantage was reduced over the 1990s. This can be seen for men by the large decrease in the positive impact of being UK born and the reversal in the sign of the marginal effect for women.

Living in London and the South East generally increases the probability that an individual has a professional/managerial position, with the impact of location tending to be greater for men than it is for women. However, there are some exceptions to this, since Black African men and women residing in London and the South East were more than 15 percentage points less likely to have a professional or managerial job than those living elsewhere in Britain. Inspection of the Controlled Access Microdata Sample (CAMS) reveals that there is considerable diversity between Black Africans by country of birth, as well as by region of residence in Britain. Over 65% of those born in South Africa and Zimbabwe living in London and the South East and elsewhere in Britain had professional/managerial jobs, compared with less than 30% for Somalians. Nigerians living outside London and the South East were much more likely to have professional or managerial occupations, while similar large discrepancies existed for migrants from Ghana and Sierra Leone. There was a higher proportion of professionals and managers among native-born Black Africans living in London and the South East than those living in other parts of Britain.

Figures L and M report the percentage in the professional/managerial social classes in different Index of Multiple Deprivation (IMD) decile areas by ethnic group.[18] The three areas reported in the figures are the most deprived, a middle-ranked and the least deprived areas. Compared with employment, it appears that the adverse impact of living in a deprived area is not as severe for most ethnic minorities. For example, many of the groups actually have a higher proportion in the professional/managerial category than the White group in the lowest IMD decile area. Although a relatively low percentage of Pakistani and Bangladeshi men in the most deprived areas had professional/managerial jobs, men from all of the other ethnic minorities living in such areas had at least the same proportion in professional/managerial occupations as the White group. Similarly for women, White women had one of the lowest proportions in professional/managerial jobs in the most deprived areas. It is also noticeable that some ethnic minorities in the least deprived areas had particularly high proportions in the professional/managerial social classes. This is true for men from the Chinese, Indian and Black African ethnic groups and Black African and Black Caribbean women.

---

[18] These figures only report raw statistics since no other controls are included.

Figure L: Percentage in the professional and managerial social classes for male ethnic groups by IMD decile, 2001

Source: 2001 CAMS

Figure M: Percentage in the professional and managerial social classes for female ethnic groups by IMD decile, 2001

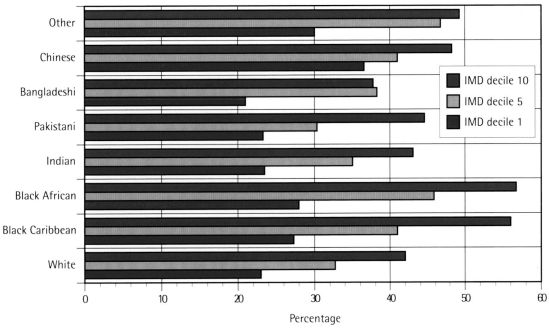

Source: 2001 CAMS

Earnings variations by ethnic group

Table 15 contains estimates from a statistical model of earnings for ethnic minorities based on pooled LFS data for men for 2002-05. Similar details are presented for women in Table 16. The information is reported as percentage differences compared with the White group, having controlled for a standard set of personal and human capital attributes.[19] The differentials are presented both with and without occupational controls, in order to detect the influence that occupation has, and also for three broad occupational groupings.

The first point to note from comparing Tables 15 and 16 is that the earnings differentials are generally much smaller for ethnic minority women than they are for men. In particular, men from each ethnic minority earn at least 10% less than the comparable White group when occupational controls are excluded, while for women, the differentials are 5% or less for three out of the seven groups. The earnings deficit was highest for Black African women at 18%, while three of the male ethnic minorities experienced more than a 20% earnings deficit. This is in accordance with earlier findings from the LFS by Leslie et al (1998), who argue that women from ethnic minority communities may not suffer from double discrimination in terms of their earnings. Including occupational controls reduces the earnings differential for each ethnic group, for both men and women, apart from the very slight increase experienced by Chinese men.[20] However, even after the inclusion of occupation, the earnings differentials for each of the male ethnic minorities remained at least 10%, whereas for women, none of the ethnic minorities experienced an earnings deficit in excess of 10%. This suggests that the earnings differentials are less about the sorting of individuals from specific groups into high- or low-paying occupations but rather about differences within occupations.

To examine this hypothesis further, we compare earnings by occupation. For men, the only ethnic minority that had an earnings advantage relative to the comparable White group was Chinese people in intermediate occupations. Again this contrasts with the situation for women, where earnings advantages are seen in four of the ethnic minority occupational groupings. In fact, Chinese women enjoyed higher earnings than the comparable White group in two out of the three occupational categories, despite suffering a small overall earnings deficit. However, for both men and women, it tends to be in the professional/ managerial occupations where the greatest earnings differentials exist. For men, only the Indian group had an earnings deficit of less than 10% in this category, whereas this was the case for five of the female ethnic minorities. Earnings differentials tend to fall with the skill level for most ethnic minorities, both for men and women. The downward earnings differential by skill relative to the White group was particularly noticeable for Black African men.

---

[19] See Appendix B for details of how the percentage differentials are calculated and the note to Table 15 for a list of the controls that were included in the models, which are based on the specifications estimated by Blackaby et al (2002).

[20] The included occupational controls are broadly defined NS-SEC categories.

Table 15: Percentage differences in earnings for men by ethnic group, 2002–05

	No occupational controls	Including occupational controls	Professional/managerial	Intermediate	Routine/semi-routine
Black Caribbean	–14.02***	–10.33***	–12.01***	–9.15**	–6.48**
Black African	–26.29***	–16.39***	–24.80***	–9.97**	–2.47
Indian	–15.13***	–11.22***	–8.61***	–12.45***	–11.13***
Pakistani	–20.47***	–14.10***	–19.43***	–15.13***	–7.87***
Bangladeshi	–27.02***	–20.71***	–24.72***	–19.18***	–17.14***
Chinese	–9.61***	–9.97***	–13.76***	2.12	–1.69
Other	–16.22***	–11.66***	–14.44***	–7.04***	–7.78***
N	54,940	54,934	26,049	13,846	15,039

Source: Labour Force Survey. © Crown copyright

Notes: Controls are included for education, experience, industry, region, sector, part–time status, firm size, immigrant cohort, job tenure and year of interview. Data relate to the working–age population.

** $p < 0.05$; *** $p < 0.01$ (two–tailed tests).

Table 16: Percentage differences in earnings for women by ethnic group, 2002–05

	No occupational controls	Including occupational controls	Professional/managerial	Intermediate	Routine/semi-routine
Black Caribbean	–5.35***	–3.25*	–6.29**	–1.00	–0.80
Black African	–17.96***	–9.88***	–15.97***	–11.31***	–1.49
Indian	–10.86***	–6.57***	–6.48***	–6.01**	–4.30*
Pakistani	–11.04***	–7.04***	–0.70	–9.61**	–5.82
Bangladeshi	–14.36**	–8.15*	–16.05**	7.57	–1.19
Chinese	–1.39	–0.70	2.33	1.82	–7.23
Other	–5.07***	–2.76**	–6.01***	–2.37	3.36
N	56,363	56,358	23,423	16,103	16,832

Source: Labour Force Survey. © Crown copyright

Notes: Controls are included for education, experience, industry, region, sector, part–time status, firm size, immigrant cohort, job tenure and year of interview. Data relate to the working–age population.

* $p < 0.1$; ** $p < 0.05$; *** $p < 0.01$ (two–tailed tests).

KEY POINTS

Most ethnic minorities experienced a faster rate of growth in the percentage of paid employees in professional/managerial occupations than the White group between 1991 and 2001. However, once personal characteristics – especially higher qualifications – are controlled for, the differentials were similar to those that existed in 1991 and the only group to have encountered much of an improvement was Black Caribbean men. Furthermore, in relative terms, men from five of the seven ethnic minorities were more likely to be in unskilled/partly skilled occupations in 2001 compared with 1991, although the opposite was true for women. Moreover, higher education graduates – especially women – appear to be finding it increasingly difficult to obtain top-level jobs. All ethnic minorities continue to have lower earnings than comparable White groups, with large earnings differentials experienced by the Black African, Pakistani and Bangladeshi groups, while in terms of earnings within occupations, the deficits tend to be largest for professional/managerial workers for virtually all of the ethnic minorities.

Conclusions

Summary of key findings

In Chapter 2 we focused on employment and argued that this is a major influence on the welfare of ethnic minorities. Over the period 1991 to 2001, there was a general improvement in employment outcomes for ethnic minorities in England and Wales. Substantial reductions in the employment gap with the White group were observed for three of the most disadvantaged groups: Black African, Pakistani and Bangladeshi men. Moreover, the narrowing of the gap for these groups was attributable in part to increased endowments of employment-enhancing characteristics, particularly educational qualifications. Other groups also experienced increased employment rates compared with the White group. However, it would be extremely misleading to suggest that such progress has eliminated ethnic minority employment disadvantage. First, in spite of increasing employment rates for most ethnic minorities, large employment deficits with the White group remained in 2001, even for those groups whose employment rates had risen. Second, Black Caribbean men, whose educational attainment lags behind all other groups, largely failed to benefit from the general improvement in the labour market, when compared with the White group. Third, convergence between the White group and ethnic minorities was much less for women than for men and the position of women from some ethnic minorities actually deteriorated. Fourth, Pakistani and Bangladeshi women continued to have extremely low employment rates in absolute terms – less than 30% for each group in 2001.

The results in Chapter 2 also demonstrated the considerable diversity of employment outcomes, not only in levels of employment rates but also in how various characteristics of individuals and their locations affect those rates. For example, we found that education was one of the strongest and most stable predictors of employment for all ethnic groups, but that the 'returns' from education, in the sense of how much it increased the likelihood of having a job, varied a lot by ethnic group. In particular, education boosted the employment chances of ethnic minorities by more than for the White group.

We also found that, where there is some variation in religion, being Muslim was associated with poorer employment outcomes for many ethnic groups and that this penalty was greater for women. Since the vast majority of Pakistanis and Bangladeshis are Muslims, it was not possible to identify a separate effect of religion for these groups. Nevertheless, part of the explanation for their lower employment rates may relate to their religious affiliation.

Another finding to emerge from Chapter 2 is that, while all ethnic groups have lower employment rates in disadvantaged areas, the size of this effect was greater for ethnic minorities. This suggests that a White individual, with a given level of human capital and other characteristics, living in an area with a particular level of deprivation, would have a higher employment rate than an identical individual from a ethnic minority in an equally deprived area. This might reflect a number of factors, including greater racial discrimination in particular types of area and the unobservable attributes of local areas and/or individuals. Taken together, our findings on education, religion and the deprived nature of neighbourhoods suggest additional sources of ethnic diversity to be aware of *and* additional mechanisms through which carefully targeted policies may reduce ethnic inequalities.

In Chapter 3 we examined self-employment and argued that, since this is an important form of activity for many ethnic groups, it must be taken into account when discussing the welfare of Britain's ethnic minorities. A focus of our research is change in the economic activity of ethnic minorities over time and, in this regard, a generally stable aggregate rate of self-employment disguised considerable ethnic variation between the Census dates. Rates of self-employment have converged somewhat for men, with increases for those groups that previously had lower self-employment rates and decreases for some of the groups with traditionally higher rates, specifically the Indians and Chinese. We argue that this is, to a large extent, consistent with the growth in the proportion of these ethnic groups who are born in the UK and the associated increase in the assimilation of the second and later generations into the education system and paid labour market. To this extent, our findings have resonance with those of Metcalf et al (1996), who, on the basis of a smaller, more detailed dataset, noted the following:

> While future self-employed need not come from the same families, the wishes of the current groups of entrepreneurs about inheritance of the business added to the idea that the very high levels of self-employment may be a passing phase. The migrant generation's employment expectations for themselves, and what they were willing to do, were very different to their aspirations for their children. They may have been willing to put family before self, and work over leisure, but few entrepreneurs felt that the business provided what they would wish for a son in his first job. (Metcalf et al, 1996, p 141)

We would argue that in the 2001 Census we have begun to see the realisation of these aspirations for the children of Indian and Chinese entrepreneurs.

The other dynamic patterns in the self-employment data are somewhat less easy to explain. While facing similar demographic changes in the composition of their group, the Pakistani and Bangladeshi groups' self-employment rates have remained broadly constant across the 1990s. This suggests the existence of other factors that are making self-employment more attractive for this group over this period. Purely on the basis of our Census data, any explanation is speculative, but three facts are worth noting. First, these groups face some of the most serious wage discrimination in the labour market. Second, they tend to be the most segregated in geographical areas with a high concentration of members of the same ethnic group.[21] Third, they are overwhelmingly Muslim, which can affect sources of business finance, types of goods and services that are sold and attitudes to entrepreneurship. These factors may help to explain their differential self-employment trends.

Chapter 3 also reveals, as in the discussion of employment, that local area effects are important. We found that both ethnically concentrated areas and those with high levels of deprivation (which are, of course, often the same places) have lower self-employment rates. Again, this relationship need not be causal but rather may reflect unobservable attributes of self-employed individuals or the local areas themselves.

In Chapter 4 we investigated the situation of ethnic minorities in employment. Over the period we examined, there was generally an improvement in the occupational distribution

---

[21] Simpson (2004) argues, however, that South Asian groups in the UK are, in fact, dispersing from highly concentrated areas.

with much higher proportions of ethnic minority workers found in managerial occupations in 2001 compared with 1991. Some of this can be explained by improvements in the distribution of characteristics, but not all. However, although investment in human capital has led to increased occupational attainment for many of the ethnic minorities compared with the White group, it is also true that a lower proportion of ethnic minority graduates are employed in professional and managerial occupations. This implies that graduates from certain groups are finding it increasingly difficult to get top-level jobs. This may in part reflect the subject choices they made at university, as evidence has shown that ethnic minorities tend to be concentrated in certain, vocationally oriented, subjects (Connor et al, 2004). Furthermore, using the most up-to-date information from the Labour Force Survey (LFS), we found that, within broad occupations, ethnic minorities still face substantial ethnic penalties in earnings even after controlling for differences in observable characteristics. Ethnic differentials are generally largest in professional and managerial occupations, which is a very broad category. The very highest earners in this category are unlikely to be from ethnic minorities – in 2004 less than 3% of FTSE 100 company directors were from a ethnic minority background (DTI, 2004). Thus, while a higher proportion of individuals from many of the ethnic minorities may be in professional and managerial occupations, those who make it into such positions do not seem to be treated the same as the White group. Earnings penalties are still a fact of life for ethnic minorities in the UK labour market.

Policy implications

The UK government's current policy efforts to combat ethnic minority disadvantage in the labour market are coordinated by the Ethnic Minority Employment Task Force, a cross-department government committee charged with fulfilling the policy objectives set out in a report by the Prime Minister's Strategy Unit (Cabinet Office, 2003). The Task Force organises its work around three main aspects: (i) *building employability* concerned with the enhancement of human capital investment by ethnic minority individuals, (ii) *connecting people to work* concerned with removing barriers to employment and (iii) *equal opportunities in the workplace* concerned with reducing employer discrimination. The second annual report of this Task Force was issued in 2006 and reported on progress so far on 28 recommendations. Of these, 20 had been either fully or partly met. In addition, the Department for Work and Pensions (DWP) has an ongoing public service agreement (PSA) target to significantly reduce the difference between the employment rates of disadvantaged groups, including ethnic minorities, and the overall rate. Other PSA targets relate to ethnic minority self-employment. In the remainder of this section we focus on six key themes, which our results suggest are important in designing policies to improve the labour market position of ethnic minorities in the UK.

(1) Taking diversity seriously

Our work confirms the importance of taking ethnic diversity seriously. For example, for Indian and Chinese men, there is very little 'problem' as far as employment penalties are concerned, while for Pakistani, Bangladeshi and Black men, these are severe. This implies the need for a more nuanced understanding of ethnic diversity where policy is concerned. In particular, the PSA targets mentioned above do not explicitly distinguish between different ethnic minorities and thus an improvement in the overall ethnic minority employment rate driven purely by changes in the position of Indian and Chinese male workers would represent only limited progress in reducing ethnic minority disadvantage. We would argue that, where targets for ethnic minority employment are set, these should adequately reflect the diversity of the labour market experiences of Britain's ethnic groups.

Targeting particular communities and providing policies that are sensitive both to their culture and needs is an efficient use of scarce government resources. To some extent this is noted in the recommendations of the Strategy Unit report (Cabinet Office, 2003). For example, the Department for Education and Skills has directed support towards Black Caribbean boys in school, as the performance of this group at GCSE level has been particularly poor, and the DWP has conducted research on the particular needs of Pakistani and Bangladeshi women who may have preferences for culturally sensitive forms of childcare. While these developments are welcome, there is more scope to tailor employment-promotion policies to particular groups, both by ethnicity and gender.

(2) Employment builds on human capital investment

A second key theme to emerge from our work is the importance of education as the key building block of employability. Educational attainment has a massive influence on the life chances of individuals and the evidence presented here suggests that the labour market returns to education are particularly high for ethnic minority workers. Of all the factors that are statistically associated with getting a job, educational attainment is the one area under the, more or less, direct control of the government and thus the area where judiciously designed policies may actually be able to make a genuine change. We saw in Chapter 2 that the improvement in the employment position of Pakistani and Black African men, relative to the White group, could be attributed in part to the improvement in their qualifications. By comparison, the Black Caribbean group failed to close the gap with the White group in either educational attainment or employment terms to anywhere near the same extent.

In this context, the Department for Education and Skills' Black Pupils Achievement Programme, which targets Black African, Black Caribbean and mixed race pupils, is a welcome development and there is some evidence that the gap between Black pupils and all pupils is closing (Ethnic Minority Employment Task Force, 2006). However, Black individuals are still more likely than those from other ethnic minorities to have dropped out of both education and the labour market at the age of 18 (Middleton et al, 2005). Recent research by Wilson et al (2005) suggests that Britain's South Asian ethnic groups outperform other groups at school largely because of their, culturally instilled, aspirations and attitudes (see also Modood, 2005). The policy challenge is to extend this success at school to other groups.

(3) Religion matters

Our regression models suggested that religion is an additional source of variation in labour market behaviour. In particular, there is some evidence that, controlling for other factors, Muslims have lower employment rates than individuals with another, or indeed no, religion. Quantifying this is problematical for some of Britain's ethnic groups simply because ethnicity and religion are highly correlated. Cultural attitudes and norms may underlie some of the low employment rates, especially for Pakistani and Bangladeshi women, but separating the influences of ethnicity and religion is extremely difficult, both conceptually and empirically. It is also true that it may be tradition, rather than religious belief per se, that influences attitudes to female labour force participation and childcare. It may also be misleading to label behaviour, such as presumably voluntary adherence to a particular religion, as a cause of economic disadvantage. The interaction between (choice of) religion and labour market success is clearly deserving of further research, a point that is emphasised by the, perhaps surprising, finding that White Muslims also experience an employment penalty, other things being equal.

From a policy perspective, given that two of the groups most disadvantaged in employment are overwhelmingly Muslim in their religious affiliation, there may be scope for government employment agencies to target resources by working more closely in the community. For example, the East London mosque successfully hosts JobCentre Plus sessions where job-search skills are taught to unemployed members of the community. Mosques and other places of worship are frequently the focus of a variety of community support activities and the provision of employment, skills or training advice in a safe and familiar setting would be a useful and relatively low-cost addition to their current activities.

(4) Neighbourhood effects

The fourth theme to emerge from our work is the importance of the local area. In the determination of both employment rates and the choice of self-employment over paid employment, ethnically diverse local area effects were found. In the case of employment, taken literally, our results suggest that a ethnic minority individual transported from a deprived area to a less deprived area would increase their chances of getting a job by more than a White person changing location in the same way. This may reflect greater levels of discrimination in poor areas or something about the nature of interactions between individuals of various ethnicities in those areas (what Borjas, 1992, calls 'ethnic capital'). On the other hand, a causal interpretation may not be warranted, as our findings could reflect unobservable differences in the characteristics of individuals in different types of area. Which of these explanations is correct matters for policy: if we accept a causal interpretation, policies aimed at reducing the general level of inequality between areas will have the beneficial side effect of reducing ethnic minority employment disadvantage. On the other hand, if the real issue is something about the characteristics of those living in poor or ethnically concentrated areas (for example, poor English language skills), policy needs to focus on improving those characteristics.

Given the importance for policy of establishing the reasons for the neighbourhood effects we find, further research on this issue is required to establish what lies behind these findings. Such research would benefit from more geographical detail in the datasets available to researchers. A considerable amount of literature now discusses neighbourhood effects (see Durlauf, 2004, for a review) and these ideas have been applied to ethnic minority labour market outcomes by Clark and Drinkwater (2002). In the UK, matching individual-level data with information that is truly relevant to the individual's *neighbourhood* is difficult. The Index of Multiple Deprivation (IMD) is a step in the right direction, as it is calculated for very small geographical areas (lower layer, Super Output Areas, as they are known). However, it is somewhat difficult to interpret. The other measures of ethnic concentration and unemployment used in our analyses were measured at local authority or higher levels of geographical aggregation and hence do not really capture what we mean by a neighbourhood. Investigation of these issues would be helped if other neighbourhood information could be mapped into the Samples of Anonymised Records (SARs). This is not currently possible, given the confidentiality requirements associated with Census data. However, more detailed data are required to establish what is really going on at the neighbourhood level.

Government policy does take some account of the geographically concentrated nature of the ethnic minority population in the UK. The DWP targets 60 'priority districts', composed of 30 areas with the highest minority concentration and the 30 with the highest unemployment rates, to encourage employment agencies to work in partnership with providers of social housing. However, the effectiveness of policy interventions may be limited if, whatever the actual ethnic concentration of an area, people have *preferences* over the ethnicities with whom they would like to interact. Clark and Drinkwater (2007: forthcoming) present evidence from the Fourth National Survey of Ethnic Minorities, which suggests that individuals who express a preference for living in areas with a majority of people of the same ethnic group have unemployment rates of up to 20 percentage points higher. These estimates control for the actual ethnic composition of where the individual lives. The tendency of some ethnic groups in the UK to exhibit 'oppositional identities' has also been noted by Battu et al (2003) and such attitudes may reduce interactions with other groups and hence limit labour market opportunities. Of course, a desire to isolate oneself from other ethnic groups may be borne of experience of discrimination or victimisation. Dustmann and Preston (2001) find that levels of discrimination against ethnic minorities are highest among the less skilled.

(5) Do we need more minority self-employment?

A fifth point emerges from our analysis of self-employment. There is a temptation to view the existence of a large ethnic entrepreneurial class as a healthy sign for the ethnic group concerned. However, two commentators on the economics of self-employment have recently asked whether more entrepreneurship is necessarily a good thing. In a provocative paper, Blanchflower (2004) argues that (i) small firms do not actually boost employment any more than large firms, (ii) self-employment does not boost macroeconomic growth rates and (iii) self-employment is stressful for those who undertake it. Similarly, Parker (2004) questions why governments in advanced economies always assume that the self-employment rate is too low. He argues that the desire to be seen supporting entrepreneurship is ideological rather than being based on a sober assessment of the costs and benefits of alternative policy interventions in the market.

In the context of ethnic minority self-employment in the UK, we would reiterate that the existence of a large proportion of an ethnic group involved in self-employment is not, of itself, an indicator of a high level of welfare for that group. The ethnic groups in the UK who are the most likely to be self-employed work the longest hours and are concentrated in unglamorous occupations earning low wages: for every Lakshmi Mittal there are thousands of takeaway owners and taxi drivers. We have argued that declining self-employment rates for Indian and Chinese groups may represent a healthy development – associated with the greater incorporation of the second generation into the paid labour market. Currently, the UK government has set the Department of Trade and Industry a PSA target to increase the self-employment rates of ethnic minorities, which are currently underrepresented in this form of activity. We believe that any policy designed to provide government support for ethnic minority entrepreneurship must ensure that due regard is paid to the quality as well as the quantity of self-employment opportunities and is not just a mechanism to provide subsidised low-quality employment to workers who would otherwise be unemployed.

(6) The persistence of discrimination

Finally, the sheer persistence of racial disadvantage in the labour market is something that emerges from our results, as well as those of many other studies. It is difficult to escape the conclusion that for some groups this reflects the discriminatory behaviour of people from other ethnicities. Daniel (1968), on the basis of 'situation tests' whereby individuals from different groups tried to access employment, accommodation and other types of service in the UK, reported how the extent of racial discrimination in employment and the provision of other services varied in extent 'from the massive to the substantial' (p 209). In the three-and-a-half decades since then, the existence of persistent, unexplainable ethnic gaps in earnings, employment and occupational attainment has been documented in scores, if not hundreds, of research papers. Recent 'audit' studies (Noon, 1993; Hoque and Noon, 1999) have shown statistically significant differences in the probability that applicants from different ethnic backgrounds obtain job interviews, while studies of attitudes show that (self-assessed) racial prejudice does exist and that its nature and extent vary in systematic ways across the characteristics of individuals (Dustmann and Preston, 2001; Heath and Cheung, 2006). Furthermore, discrimination need not be overt or deliberate. Roberts and Campbell (2006) show how interviewers may inadvertently disadvantage those from ethnic minorities and how the characteristics of interviewees that are not actually relevant to the job may adversely influence the outcome of job interviews for ethnic minority individuals.

In this context, a range of policies to combat direct discrimination is possible. The 2000 Race Relations (Amendment) Act imposed a statutory requirement on public sector bodies to promote racial equality. Heath and Cheung (2006) suggest that this could be extended to the private sector, although these authors also note that it is too early to evaluate the Act's impact on the public sector. Much more interventionist policies are also possible, including the imposition of racial quotas on employers. However, there is unlikely to be the political will for this controversial idea. Perhaps more acceptable are policies requiring those who tender for public sector contracts to strive for certain standards of racial equality. Such policies have contributed to improved employment rates for Black people in the US (Darity and Mason, 1998) and are set to be piloted in the UK. Whether by themselves such policies are able to reduce the significant and persistent employment and earnings differentials documented in this report remains to be seen.

Final thoughts

Two underlying ideas have motivated our analysis of Census microdata in this report. First, that the full *diversity* of the labour market experiences of ethnic minorities in Britain needs to be taken into account and, second, that the *dynamic* patterns and trends in ethnic employment need to be understood as different from those of the majority community. Diversity in employment outcomes exists between ethnic groups and genders, but also in how, and to what extent, those outcomes are explained by the observable characteristics of the different groups. Similarly, dynamic patterns are found to be heterogeneous, contributing to increasing or decreasing ethnic inequality in different contexts. Thus, effective labour market policy targeted at improving the welfare of ethnic minorities in Britain must take account of the diversity of these groups, as well as how their current labour market situation has evolved over time.

References

Ajayi-Obe, O. and Parker, S. (2005) 'The changing nature of work among the self-employed in the 1990s: evidence from Britain', *Journal of Labor Research*, vol 26, pp 501-17.

Aldrich, H., Cater, J., Jones, T. and McEvoy, D. (1981) 'Business development and self-segregation: Asian enterprise in three British cities', in C. Peach, V. Robinson and S. Smith (eds) *Ethnic Segregation in Cities*, London: Croom Helm, pp 170-90.

Alvarez, R.M. and Nagler, J. (1998) 'When models and politics collide: estimating models of multiparty elections', *American Journal of Political Science*, 42, pp 55-96.

Arulampalam, W., Gregg, P. and Gregory, M. (2001), 'Unemployment scarring', *Economic Journal*, vol 111, pp 577-84.

Autor, D.H., Levy, F. and Murnane, R.J. (2003) 'The skill content of recent technological change: an empirical exploration', *Quarterly Journal of Economics*, vol 118, pp 1279-333.

Bank of England (1999) *The Financing of Ethnic Minority Firms in the United Kingdom*, London: Bank of England, p 21.

Battu, H. and Sloane, P. (2004) 'Over-education and ethnic minorities in Britain', *Manchester School*, vol 72, pp 535-59.

Battu, H., Mwale, M. and Zenou, Y. (2003) 'Do oppositional identities reduce employment for ethnic minorities?', IZA Discussion Paper No. 721, Bonn: IZA.

Blackaby, D.H., Clark, K., Leslie, D.G. and Murphy, P.D. (1994) 'Black–white male earnings and employment prospects in the 1970s and 1980s: evidence for Britain', *Economics Letters*, vol 46, pp 273-9.

Blackaby, D.H., Drinkwater, S.J., Leslie, D.G. and Murphy, P.D. (1997) 'A picture of male and female unemployment amongst ethnic minorities in Britain', *Scottish Journal of Political Economy*, vol 44, pp 182-97.

Blackaby, D.H., Leslie, D.G., Murphy, P.D. and O'Leary, N.C. (1999) 'Unemployment among Britain's ethnic minorities', *Manchester School*, vol 67, pp 1-20.

Blackaby, D.H., Leslie, D.G., Murphy, P.D. and O'Leary, N.C. (2002) 'White/ethnic minority and employment differentials in Britain: evidence from the LFS', *Oxford Economic Papers*, vol 54, pp 270-97.

Blanchflower, D. (2004) 'Self-employment: more may not be better', NBER Working Paper No. 10286, Cambridge, MA: National Bureau of Economic Research.

Blanden, J. and Gibbons, S. (2006) *The Persistence of Poverty Across Generations: A View from Two British Cohorts*, Bristol/York: The Policy Press/Joseph Rowntree Foundation.

Bonin, H., Constant, A., Tatsiramos, K. and Zimmermann, K. (2006) 'Native–migrant differences in risk attitudes', IZA Discussion Paper No. 1999, Bonn: IZA.

Borjas, G. (1992) 'Ethnic capital and intergenerational mobility', *Quarterly Journal of Economics*, vol 107, pp 123-50.

Borooah, V. (2001) 'How do employees of ethnic origin fare on the occupational ladder in Britain?', *Scottish Journal of Political Economy*, vol 48, pp 1-26.

Brown, C. (1984) *Black and White Britain*, London: Heinemann.

Brown, M. (2000) 'Religion and economic activity in the South Asian population', *Ethnic and Racial Studies*, vol 23, pp 1035-61.

Cabinet Office (2003) *Ethnic Minorities and the Labour Market, Final Report*, London: Prime Minister's Strategy Unit.

Carmichael, F. and Woods, R. (2000) 'Ethnic penalties in unemployment and occupational attainment: evidence from Britain', *International Review of Applied Economics*, vol 14, pp 71-98.

Clark, A. and Oswald, A. (1994) 'Unhappiness and unemployment', *Economic Journal*, vol 104, pp 648-59.

Clark, K. and Drinkwater, S. (1998) 'Ethnicity and self-employment in Britain', *Oxford Bulletin of Economics and Statistics*, vol 60, pp 383-407.

Clark, K. and Drinkwater, S. (2000) 'Pushed in or pulled out? Self-employment among ethnic minorities in England and Wales', *Labour Economics*, vol 7, pp 603-28.

Clark, K. and Drinkwater, S. (2002) 'Enclaves, neighbourhood effects and economic activity: ethnic minorities in England and Wales', *Journal of Population Economics*, vol 15, pp 5-30.

Clark, K. and Drinkwater, S. (2005) 'Dynamics and diversity: ethnic employment differences in England and Wales, 1991-2001', IZA Discussion Paper No. 1698, Bonn: IZA.

Clark, K. and Drinkwater, S. (2007: forthcoming) 'Segregation preferences and labour market outcomes', *Economics Letters*.

Clark, K., Drinkwater, S. and Leslie, D. (1998) 'Ethnicity and self-employment earnings in Britain, 1973-95', *Applied Economics Letters*, vol 5, pp 631-4.

Connor, H., Tyers, C., Modood, T. and Hillage, J. (2004) 'Why the difference? A closer look at higher education ethnic minority students and graduates', Department for Education and Skills Research Report RR552, Brighton: Institute for Employment Studies.

Daly, M. (1991) 'The 1980s – a decade of growth in enterprise', *Employment Gazette*, vol 99, pp 109-34.

Daniel, W. (1968) *Racial Discrimination in England*, London: Penguin.

Darity, W. and Mason, P. (1998) 'Evidence on discrimination in employment: codes of color, codes of gender', *Journal of Economic Perspectives*, vol 12, pp 63-90.

Disney, R. (1999) 'Why have older men stopped working?', in P. Gregg and J. Wadsworth (eds) *The State of Working Britain*, Manchester: Manchester University Press, pp 58-74.

Drew, D. (1995) *'Race', Education and Work: The Statistics of Inequality*, Aldershot: Avebury Press.

DTI (Department of Trade and Industry) (2004) *2004 Ethnic Minority Directors Index: FTSE 100 Companies*, London: DTI (www.dti.gov.uk/files/file13426.pdf).

Durlauf, S. (2004) 'Neighborhood effects', in V. Henderson and J.-F. Thisse (eds) *Handbook of Regional and Urban Economics, Volume 4: Cities and Geography*, Amsterdam: North-Holland.

Dustmann, C. and Preston, I. (2001) 'Attitudes to ethnic minorities, ethnic context and location decisions', *Economic Journal*, vol 111, pp 353-73.

DWP (Department for Work and Pensions) (2001) *UK Employment Action Plan 2001*, London: DWP.

DWP (2004) *Equality. Opportunity. Success*, Ethnic Minority Employment Task Force Year 1 Progress Report, London: DWP (www.emetaskforce.gov.uk/pdf/EMETF.pdf).

Ethnic Minority Employment Task Force (2006) *Second Annual Report*. London: EMETF.

Even, E. and MacPherson, D. (1993) 'The decline of private-sector unionism and the gender wage gap', *Journal of Human Resources*, vol 28, pp 279-96.

Freeman, R. (1999) 'The economics of crime', in O. Ashenfelter and D. Card (eds) *Handbook of Labor Economics*, Amsterdam: North-Holland, pp 3529-71.

Gomulka, J and Stern, N. (1990) 'The employment of married women in the United Kingdom 1970-83', *Economica*, vol 57, pp 171-99.

Goos, M. and Manning, A. (2003) 'Lousy and lovely jobs: the rising polarization of work in Britain', Centre for Economic Performance Discussion Paper No. 604, London: CEP.

Green, F. and McIntosh, S. (2006: forthcoming) 'Is there a genuine under-utilisation of skills amongst the over-qualified?', *Applied Economics*.

Greene, W.H. (2003) *Econometric Analysis* (5th edn), Upper Saddle River, NJ: Prentice-Hall.

Gregg, P. and Wadsworth, J. (2004) 'Two sides to every story: measuring the polarization of work', Centre for Economic Performance Discussion Paper No, 632, London: CEP.

Halvorsen, R. and Palmquist, R. (1980) 'The interpretation of dummy variables in semilogarithmic equations', *American Economic Review*, vol 70, pp 474-5.

Heath, A. and Cheung, S.Y. (2006) 'Ethnic penalties in the labour market: employers and discrimination', Department for Work and Pensions Research Report No 341, London: DWP.

Heath, A. and McMahon, D. (1997) 'Education and occupational attainments: the impact of ethnic origins', in V. Karn (ed) *Ethnicity in the 1991 Census, Volume 4, Education, Employment and Housing*, London: HMSO, pp 91-113.

Heath, A. and Yu, S. (2005), 'Explaining ethnic minority disadvantage', in A. Heath, J. Ermisch and D. Gallie (eds) *Understanding Social Change*, Oxford: Oxford University Press, pp 187-224.

Heath, A., McMahon, D. and Roberts, J. (2000) 'Ethnic differences in the labour market: a comparison of the Sample Anonymised Records and Labour Force Survey', *Journal of the Royal Statistical Society Series A*, vol 163, pp 341-61.

Hoque, K. and Noon, M. (1999) 'Racial discrimination in speculative applications: new optimism six years on?', *Human Resource Management Journal*, vol 9, pp 71-82.

Holdsworth, C. and Dale, A. (1997) 'Ethnic differences in women's employment', *Work, Employment and Society*, vol 11, pp 435-57.

Huber, P.J. (1967) 'The behavior of maximum likelihood estimates under non-standard conditions', Proceedings of the Fifth Berkeley Symposium on Mathematical Statistics, Berkeley, CA: University of California Press.

Jones, T., Ram, M. and Edwards, P. (2006) 'Ethnic minority business and the employment of illegal immigrants', *Entrepreneurship and Regional Development*, vol 18, pp 133-50.

Leslie, D. and Drinkwater, S. (1999) 'Staying on in full-time education: reasons for higher participation rates among ethnic minority men and women', *Economica*, vol 66, pp 63-77.

Leslie, D., Drinkwater, S. and O'Leary, N. (1998) 'Unemployment and earnings among Britain's ethnic minorities: some signs for optimism', *Ethnic and Racial Studies*, vol 24, pp 489-506.

Leslie, D., Lindley, J. and Thomas, L. (2002) 'Who did worse? A comparison of US and British non-white unemployment 1970-1998', *Applied Economics*, vol 34, pp 1041-54.

Lindley, J. (2002) 'Race or religion? The impact of religion on the employment and earnings of Britain's ethnic communities', *Journal of Ethnic and Migration Studies*, vol 28, pp 427-42.

Mansaray, A. (2003) 'Review essay: the alchemy of mixed race', *The Global Review of Ethnopolitics*, vol 2, pp 100-6.

Metcalf, H., Modood, T. and Virdee, S. (1996) *Asian Self-Employment: The Interaction of Culture and Economics in England*, London: Policy Studies Institute.

Middleton, S., Rennison, J., Cebulla, A., Perren, K. and De-Beaman, S. (2005) *Young People from Ethnic Minority Backgrounds: Evidence from the Education Maintenance Allowance Pilots Database*, Department for Education and Skills Research Report RR627, Loughborough: DfES.

Modell, S. (1999) 'Ethnic inequality in England: an analysis based on the 1991 Census', *Ethnic and Racial Studies*, vol 22, pp 966-89.

Modood, T. (2005) 'The educational attainments of ethnic minorities in Britain', in G. Loury, T. Modood and S. Teles (eds) *Ethnicity, Social Mobility and Public Policy: Comparing the US and UK*, Cambridge: Cambridge University Press, pp 288-308.

Nickell, S. (2004) 'Poverty and worklessness in Britain', *Economic Journal*, vol 114, pp C1-C25.

Noon, M. (1993) 'Racial discrimination in speculative applications: evidence from the UK's top 100 firms', *Human Resource Management Journal*, vol 3, pp 35-47.

Oaxaca, R. (1973) 'Male–female wage differentials in urban labor markets', *International Economic Review*, vol 14, pp 693-709.

OECD (Organisation for Economic Co-operation and Development) (2003) 'Statistical annex', in *OECD Employment Outlook 2003*, Paris: OECD.

ONS (Office for National Statistics) (2005) *The National Statistics Socio-economic Classification User Manual*, London: ONS.

ONS (2006) *A Guide to Comparing 1991 and 2001 Census Ethnic Group Data*, London: ONS.

Parker, S. (2004) *The Economics of Self-Employment and Entrepreneurship*, Cambridge: Cambridge University Press.

Parker, S., Belghitar, Y. and Barmby, T. (2005) 'Wage uncertainty and the labour supply of self-employed workers', *Economic Journal*, vol 115, pp C190-C207.

Platt, L. (2005a) 'The intergenerational social mobility of minority ethnic groups', *Sociology*, vol 39, pp 445-61.

Platt, L. (2005b) *Migration and Social Mobility: The Life Chances of Britain's Ethnic Communities*, Bristol/York: The Policy Press/Joseph Rowntree Foundation.

Roberts, C. and Campbell, S. (2006) *Talk on Trial: Job Interviews, Language and Ethnicity*, DWP Research Report No. 344, London: DWP.

Robinson, P. (1988) 'Root-N consistent semi-parametric estimation', *Econometrica*, vol 56, pp 931-54.

Simpson, L. (2004) 'Statistics of racial segregation: measures, evidence and policy', *Urban Studies*, vol 41, pp 661-81.

Simpson, L. and Akinwale, B. (2004) 'Quantifying stability and change in ethnic group', Mimeo, Centre for Census and Survey Research, University of Manchester (www.ccsr.ac.uk/staff/Ludi/documents/JOSstability.pdf).

Simpson, L., Purdam, K., Tajar, A., Fieldhouse, E., Gavalas, V., Tranmer, M., Pritchard, J. and Dorling, D. (2006) *Ethnic Minority Populations and the Labour Market: An Analysis of the 1991 and 2001 Census*, DWP Research Report No. 333, London: DWP.

Smith, D.J. (1976) *The Facts of Racial Disadvantage: A National Survey*, London: Political and Economic Planning.

Stewart, M.B. (1983) 'Racial discrimination and occupational attainment in Britain', *Economic Journal*, vol 93, pp 521-41.

Weir, G. (2003) 'Self-employment in the UK labour market', *Labour Market Trends*, September, pp 441-51.

White, H. (1980) 'A heteroskedasticity-consistent covariance matrix estimator and a direct test for heteroskedasticity', *Econometrica*, vol 48, pp 817-38.

Wilson, D., Burgess, S. and Briggs, A. (2005) 'The dynamics of school attainment of England's ethnic minorities', CMPO Working Paper Series No. 05/130, Bristol: University of Bristol.

Yatchew, A. (2003) *Semi-parametric Estimation for the Applied Econometrician*, Cambridge: Cambridge University Press.

Appendix A: Data appendix

Ethnic group

The ethnicity question in the 1991 Census asked the person to tick the appropriate box from the following options:

- ☐ 0 White
- ☐ 1 Black Caribbean
- ☐ 2 Black African
- ☐ 3 Black-Other (please describe)
- ☐ 4 Indian
- ☐ 5 Pakistani
- ☐ 6 Bangladeshi
- ☐ 7 Chinese
- ☐ Any other ethnic group (please describe)

The question also stated that: 'If the person is descended from more than one ethnic or racial group, please tick the group to which the person considers he/she belongs, or tick the 'Any other ethnic group' box and describe the person's ancestry in the space provided'.

The ethnicity question in the 2001 Census asked the person to choose *one* section from A to E, then tick the appropriate box to indicate their cultural background:

A White
- ☐ British
- ☐ Irish
- ☐ Any other White background (please write in)

B Mixed
- ☐ White and Black Caribbean
- ☐ White and Black African
- ☐ White and Asian
- ☐ Any other Mixed background (please write in)

C Asian or Asian British
- ☐ Indian
- ☐ Pakistani
- ☐ Bangladeshi
- ☐ Any other Asian background (please write in)

D Black or Black British
- ☐ Caribbean
- ☐ African
- ☐ Any other Black background (please write in)

E Chinese or other ethnic group
- ☐ Chinese
- ☐ Any other (please write in)

Economic activity

The economic activity question in the 1991 Census asked which of the following things was the person doing last week (more than one option could be chosen):

☐ 1 Was working for an employer full time (more than 30 hours a week)
☐ 2 Was working for an employer part time (one hour or more a week)
☐ 3 Was self-employed, employing other people
☐ 4 Was self-employed, not employing other people
☐ 5 Was on a government employment or training scheme
☐ 6 Was waiting to start a job he/she had already accepted
☐ 7 Was unemployed and looking for a job
☐ 8 Was at school or in full-time education
☐ 9 Was unable to work because of long-term sickness or disability
☐ 10 Was retired from paid work
☐ 11 Was looking after the home or family
☐ Other (please specify)

From the responses to these questions, the following categories were created to described the respondent's primary economic position in the 1991 Samples of Anonymised Records (SARs):

☐ 1 Full-time employee
☐ 2 Part-time employee
☐ 3 Self-employed, with employees
☐ 4 Self-employed, no employees
☐ 5 On a government scheme
☐ 6 Unemployed
☐ 7 Student
☐ 8 Permanently sick
☐ 9 Retired
☐ 10 Other

Economic outcomes were derived from the above categories as follows:

- Activity rate = $((1+2+3+4+5+6)/(1+2+3+4+5+6+7+8+9+10))*100$
- Employment rate = $((1+2+3+4+5)/(1+2+3+4+5+6+7+8+9+10))*100$
- Employment rate (no students) = $((1+2+3+4+5)/(1+2+3+4+5+6+8+9+10))*100$
- Unemployment rate = $(6/(1+2+3+4+5+6))*100$

The following economic activity questions were asked in the 2001 Census:

18 Last week, were you doing any paid work:
- as an employee, or on a government-sponsored scheme;
- as a self-employed/freelance, or in your own/family business?

(Tick 'Yes' if away from work ill, on maternity leave, on holiday or temporarily laid off. Tick 'Yes' for any paid work, including casual or temporary work, even if for only one hour. Tick 'Yes' if you worked, paid or unpaid, in your own/family business.)

Yes → go to Question 24
No → go to Question 19

19 Were you actively looking for any kind of work during the last 4 weeks?
☐ Yes or ☐ No

20 If a job had been available last week, could you have started it within 2 weeks?
    ☐ Yes   or   ☐ No

21 Last week, were you waiting to start a job already obtained?
    ☐ Yes   or   ☐ No

22 Last week, were you any of the following? (tick all the boxes that apply)
    ☐ Retired
    ☐ Student
    ☐ Looking after home/family
    ☐ Permanently sick/disabled
    ☐ None of the above

The change in the nature of the economic activity questions to some extent reflected the intention to make the statistics compatible with the International Labour Office (ILO) definition of economic status.

From the responses to these questions, the following categories could be identified in the 2001 SARs:

1 Employee part time
2 Employee full time
3 Self-employed with employees – part time
4 Self-employed with employees – full time
5 Self-employed without employees – part time
6 Self-employed without employees – full time
7 Unemployed, seeking work and available to start within 2 weeks
8 Unemployed, waiting to start a job already obtained and available to start within 2 weeks
9 Retired
10 Student (not economically active)
11 Looking after the home or family
12 Permanently sick or disabled
13 Other

Students who were economically active were coded in categories 1-8 above if they reported that they did some form of economic activity.

Economic outcomes were derived from the above questions as follows:

- Activity rate = $((1+2+3+4+5+6+7+8)/(1+2+3+4+5+6+7+8+9+10+11+12+13))*100$
- Employment rate = $((1+2+3+4+5+6)/(1+2+3+4+5+6+7+8+9+10+11+12+13))*100$
- Employment rate (no students) = $((1+2+3+4+5+6)/(1+2+3+4+5+6+7+8+9+11+12+13))*100$. *Note:* All full-time students are removed from both the numerator and denominator under this definition, that is, economically active students are excluded from this definition.
- Unemployment rate = $((7+8)/(1+2+3+4+5+6+7+8))*100$

Information on selected explanatory variables

- *Higher qualifications*: An individual was identified as having a higher qualification in 1991 if they responded that they had any post-school qualification. In 2001, those with level 4 or level 5 qualifications were deemed to have a higher qualification. Level 4/5 qualifications refer to first degree; higher degree; NVQ levels 4 and 5; HNC; HND;

qualified teacher status; qualified medical doctor; qualified dentist; qualified nurse; midwife; health visitor.

- *Dependent children in household:* In both years, residents of communal establishments were defined as having no dependent children in their household.
- For the 2001 SARs and CAMS we use the data with imputed values included.
- *Index of Multiple Deprivation (IMD):* Published by the Office of the Deputy Prime Minister. The IMD is constructed using seven Super Output Area Level domain indicies. These domains are income deprivation; employment deprivation; health deprivation and disability; education, skills and training deprivation; barriers to housing and services; crime and living environment deprivation. The indicators used to construct the domains generally relate to 2001. It should be noted that the IMD scores for England and Wales are constructed slightly differently. The IMD is only available in the CAMS, since no local authority identifiers are present in the 2001 individual Licensed SARs, which are available through the Centre for Census and Survey Research at the University of Manchester.

Appendix B:
Econometric models

Most of the econometric models in the report use the probit estimator (see Greene, 2003, p 710), whereby the dependent variable either takes a value of 0 or 1, such as if the individual is either employed or not employed. We estimate the parameters of the following binary probit model:

$$E_i^* = x_i' \beta + u_i$$

where x_i is a vector of explanatory variables, β a vector of associated coefficients and u_i a standard normal random error term. The binary dependent variable indicating a particular state (for example, is employed) is defined as follows:

$$E_i = 1 \text{ if } E_i^* \geq 0, \text{ the individual is in employment}$$

$$E_i = 0 \text{ otherwise, the individual is out of employment}$$

Rather than reporting coefficients from the probit models, which are not straightforward to interpret, *marginal effects* have been computed for the probit estimates. Multiplying these marginal effects by 100 will then provide the percentage-point difference in the predicted probability of a strictly positive outcome (is employed) between two categories, if the explanatory variable is categorical, or for a marginal increment to a continuous explanatory variable, holding all other factors constant. The tables in the report also contain asterisks to indicate significance levels. The significance levels are calculated using heteroscedasticity robust standard errors (Huber, 1967; White, 1980).

The decomposition using the probit model is based on Gomulka and Stern (1990) and can be specified as follows:[22]

$$\hat{E}^w - \hat{E}^j = \{\bar{P}(x^w\hat{\beta}^*) - \bar{P}(x^j\hat{\beta}^*)\} + \{[\bar{P}(x^w\hat{\beta}^w) - \bar{P}(x^w\hat{\beta}^*)] - [\bar{P}(x^j\hat{\beta}^j) - \bar{P}(x^j\hat{\beta}^*)]\}$$

where $\hat{E}^w$ is the average of the predicted probabilities (for example, for employment) for the White group and $\hat{E}^j$ is the same for the ethnic minority j. $\hat{\beta}$ is the vector of estimated coefficients from the probit model and $\hat{\beta}^*$ is a vector of estimated coefficients from a probit model estimated on a pooled sample (the White and the ethnic minority comparison group), $\bar{P}(x^j\hat{\beta}^j)$ is the average of the fitted probabilities from the probit model estimated using the observations in group j and the estimated coefficients from group j and so on. The first term in the braces is the component of the probability difference due to observed characteristics, while the second term in braces is the effect of coefficients, which corresponds to unobservable, group-specific influences on the employment probability. The decomposition allows us to estimate what proportion of the difference between any ethnic minority and the White majority is due to differences in observed characteristics. The remaining 'unexplained' component may reflect differential treatment by the labour market, such as employer discrimination, cultural/ethnic differences in motivation or preferences between groups.

---

[22] This is as implemented in Blackaby et al (2002) and is basically an extension of the Oaxaca (1973) decomposition to the case of a binary-dependent variable.

A version of this decomposition is used in Chapter 3 to decompose within-group differences over time in the probability of self-employment. This uses the same equation as above but the superscript w refers to 2001 and j to 1991.

The following wage equation is estimated in Chapter 4:

$$\log w_i = X_i'\beta + \sum_{j=1}^{8} \gamma_j D_{ji} + \varepsilon_i$$

where w_i is the wage of individual i, X_i is a vector of personal characteristics, β is a vector of coefficients, D_{ji} contains a set of eight ethnic dummy variables and γ_j their associated coefficients and ε_i is an error term. The wage differential (in percentage terms) relative to the White group ($j = 1$) can then be calculated using the following formula (Halvorsen and Palmquist, 1980):

$$D_j^* = [\exp(\hat{\gamma}_j) - 1] \times 100$$

where $\hat{\gamma}_j$ represents the estimated coefficient for ethnic group j.

Appendix C: Additional data analysis and econometric estimates

Table A1: Employment rates (no students) and sample sizes for men and women by narrow ethnic group in England and Wales, 2001 and 2002–05

| | Male | | | | Female | | | |
| | CAMS | | LFS | | CAMS | | LFS | |
	Rate	N	Rate	N	Rate	N	Rate	N
White British	81.2	416,391	82.6	93,656	72.0	377,910	73.6	89,817
Other White	80.6	12,527	80.6	4,224	67.9	13,602	69.8	4,338
White & Black Caribbean	68.8	1,099	75.0	164	60.1	1,207	64.7	232
White & Black African	64.0	528	76.3	76	60.6	513	66.3	98
White & Asian	77.5	1,072	67.1	152	65.2	1,068	71.1	149
Other Mixed	73.6	903	72.0	132	65.1	1,011	70.4	172
Indian	80.5	9,306	82.4	2,275	65.2	9,087	63.1	2,285
Pakistani	66.4	5,515	70.7	1,445	27.4	5,525	24.8	1,537
Bangladeshi	63.3	2,077	67.3	480	22.2	2,035	20.6	545
Other Asian	73.6	2,510	77.1	610	55.7	1,826	57.4	678
Black Caribbean	68.9	4,832	72.0	942	71.0	5,507	69.3	1,119
Black African	72.0	3,542	76.5	817	58.8	3,824	56.4	1,070
Other Black	67.8	661	76.0	96	64.2	759	67.7	102
Chinese	82.4	1,723	84.4	360	66.7	1,958	65.2	439
Other ethnic group	71.3	1,632	69.9	1,088	55.5	2,356	49.4	1,177

Source: 2001 Census, CAMS and 2002-05 Labour Force Survey (pooled). © Crown copyright

Table A2: Probit estimates of employment incidence, detailed specification: 2001

	Men			Women		
	Mean	M. E.	S. E.	Mean	M. E.	S. E.
Age	40.913	0.026	0.000	39.128	0.036	0.001
Age squared/100	18.340	-0.036	0.000	16.590	-0.047	0.001
Married	0.455	0.116	0.002	0.465	0.005	0.002
Remarried	0.081	0.092	0.002	0.080	0.020	0.003
Separated	0.024	0.045	0.003	0.036	-0.022	0.004
Divorced	0.085	0.036	0.002	0.109	0.016	0.003
Widowed	0.009	0.026	0.005	0.019	-0.068	0.006
Only dependent children in household	0.325	0.001	0.001	0.427	-0.209	0.002
Non-dependent children in household	0.024	-0.006	0.004	0.024	-0.082	0.005
Dependent and non-dependent children	0.023	0.025	0.003	0.021	0.029	0.005
Level 1 qualifications	0.191	0.076	0.001	0.199	0.137	0.002
Level 2 qualifications	0.183	0.086	0.001	0.220	0.183	0.002
Level 3 qualifications	0.073	0.095	0.001	0.078	0.201	0.002
Level 4/5 qualifications	0.218	0.109	0.001	0.221	0.229	0.002
Other qualifications	0.092	0.071	0.001	0.047	0.118	0.003
UK born	0.902	0.003	0.003	0.890	0.047	0.004
White Irish	0.013	-0.031	0.006	0.013	0.005	0.007
Other White	0.027	-0.054	0.005	0.031	-0.065	0.006
Mixed: White & Black Caribbean	0.002	-0.125	0.014	0.003	-0.087	0.014
Mixed: White & Black African	0.001	-0.181	0.022	0.001	-0.079	0.022
Mixed: White & Asian	0.002	-0.049	0.013	0.002	-0.069	0.016
Other Mixed	0.002	-0.091	0.016	0.002	-0.056	0.016
Indian	0.020	-0.018	0.008	0.021	-0.003	0.010
Pakistani	0.012	-0.045	0.008	0.013	-0.141	0.011
Bangladeshi	0.004	-0.065	0.011	0.005	-0.143	0.016
Other Asian	0.005	-0.083	0.011	0.004	-0.061	0.014
Black Caribbean	0.010	-0.109	0.007	0.013	0.019	0.007
Black African	0.008	-0.185	0.010	0.009	-0.085	0.009
Other Black	0.001	-0.144	0.019	0.002	-0.036	0.018
Chinese	0.004	-0.031	0.011	0.005	-0.018	0.012
Other ethnic group	0.003	-0.131	0.013	0.005	-0.116	0.012
Christian	0.682	0.018	0.002	0.737	0.028	0.002
Buddhist	0.003	-0.030	0.011	0.003	-0.050	0.014
Hindu	0.011	-0.013	0.009	0.011	0.031	0.011
Jewish	0.005	0.037	0.008	0.005	-0.036	0.011
Muslim	0.027	-0.115	0.008	0.027	-0.180	0.009
Sikh	0.006	-0.046	0.012	0.007	0.050	0.012
Other religion	0.018	0.009	0.004	0.010	-0.006	0.008
Religion not stated	0.073	-0.014	0.003	0.063	-0.014	0.003
North East	0.048	-0.013	0.003	0.049	-0.005	0.004
North West	0.128	0.015	0.002	0.128	0.026	0.003
Yorkshire and the Humber	0.094	0.032	0.002	0.094	0.040	0.004
East Midlands	0.081	0.046	0.002	0.080	0.035	0.004
West Midlands	0.101	0.043	0.002	0.099	0.031	0.004
East of England	0.105	0.066	0.002	0.104	0.026	0.004
South East	0.155	0.066	0.002	0.154	0.028	0.003
South West	0.093	0.050	0.002	0.092	0.023	0.004
Inner London	0.055	0.024	0.003	0.058	-0.021	0.005
Outer London	0.084	0.054	0.002	0.089	0.019	0.004
In fairly good health	0.207	-0.118	0.002	0.240	-0.110	0.002
In not good health	0.085	-0.531	0.003	0.081	-0.464	0.003
Index of Multiple Deprivation/100	0.212	-0.079	0.003	0.215	-0.127	0.005
Pseudo R^2		0.239			0.159	
N		470,603			433,754	

Source: 2001 Census, CAMS. © Crown copyright

Notes: Default categories are single, no children in household, born overseas, no qualifications, White British, no religion, lives in Wales and in good health. All full-time students have been excluded from the analysis. The table contains marginal effects (M. E.) and heteroscedasticity robust standard errors (S. E.) as well as the means of the explanatory variables.

Table A3: Marginal effects on the probability of self-employment, 1991 and 2001

	Male	Female
Age 20-24	0.127***	0.062***
Age 25-29	0.216***	0.112***
Age 30-44	0.250***	0.127***
Age 45-59	0.315***	0.162***
Age 60-65	0.395***	–
Higher qualifications	–0.047***	0.002***
Single	–0.032***	–0.003***
Married	–0.019***	0.008***
Dependent children	0.026***	0.014***
UK born	–0.012***	–0.016***
Long-term illness	0.013***	0.015***
Owns, mortgage	–0.050***	–0.022***
Social renter	–0.092***	–0.047***
Other renter	–0.035***	–0.006***
Black Caribbean	–0.086***	–0.043***
Black African	–0.048***	–0.024***
Indian	0.039***	0.028***
Pakistani	0.077***	0.121***
Bangladeshi	0.013	0.056
Chinese	0.159***	0.100***
Other	–0.035***	–0.014***
White*2001	–0.005***	0.007***
Black Caribbean*2001	0.061***	0.033**
Black African*2001	0.023	–0.000
Indian*2001	–0.012*	–0.007*
Pakistani*2001	0.014	–0.032***
Bangladeshi*2001	0.020	–0.028*
Chinese*2001	–0.042***	–0.009
Other*2001	0.038***	0.019**
North	–0.022***	–0.004**
Yorkshire & Humberside	0.010***	0.006***
East Midlands	0.010***	0.007***
East Anglia	0.038***	0.013***
Inner London	0.077***	0.058***
Outer London	0.047***	0.006***
Rest of South East	0.039***	0.015***
South West	0.059***	0.027***
West Midlands	0.008***	0.003*
North West	0.008***	0.002
Wales	0.034***	0.010***
N	677,142	546,636

Source: 1991 and 2001 Census, SARs (pooled). © Crown copyright

Notes: * $p < 0.1$; ** $p < 0.05$; *** $p < 0.01$ (two-tailed tests).

Table A4: Social class for men by ethnic group, 1991 and 2001

	White		Black Caribbean		Black African		Indian		Pakistani		Bangladeshi		Chinese		Other	
	1991	2001	1991	2001	1991	2001	1991	2001	1991	2001	1991	2001	1991	2001	1991	2001
Professional	7.11	6.37	2.94	4.22	13.94	10.90	12.07	11.99	7.64	8.03	5.34	5.00	22.72	19.33	13.50	10.76
Managerial	29.77	33.78	15.68	28.86	23.51	34.25	22.68	34.34	16.19	22.53	10.39	17.85	26.00	32.03	33.78	34.78
Skilled non-manual	11.44	14.59	12.16	16.90	18.73	19.41	15.36	18.08	13.34	18.95	8.01	14.54	10.30	13.45	16.01	18.66
Skilled manual	31.09	28.08	37.18	29.04	16.73	15.43	24.45	17.93	29.33	20.43	32.64	20.11	28.34	10.55	19.53	17.72
Partly skilled	15.98	11.31	24.15	14.90	18.13	14.51	20.70	13.61	27.19	23.65	38.58	40.04	10.07	22.97	13.29	13.67
Unskilled	4.61	5.87	7.90	6.01	8.96	5.49	4.74	4.06	6.31	6.40	5.04	2.46	2.58	1.68	3.90	4.40
N	201,023	320,191	1,735	2,893	502	2,184	2,826	5,880	982	2,765	337	1,059	427	1,071	1,874	5,112

Source: 1991 and 2001 Census, SARs. © Crown copyright

Table A5: Social class for women by ethnic group, 1991 and 2001

	White		Black Caribbean		Black African		Indian		Pakistani		Bangladeshi		Chinese		Other	
	1991	2001	1991	2001	1991	2001	1991	2001	1991	2001	1991	2001	1991	2001	1991	2001
Professional	1.79	3.23	1.13	3.39	2.20	6.15	4.26	7.77	1.76	4.94	3.08	4.71	9.09	12.01	3.95	5.95
Managerial	27.51	30.69	33.58	36.66	34.07	35.49	17.36	25.06	20.29	24.06	23.08	23.29	32.05	32.79	31.48	34.51
Skilled non-manual	40.10	39.23	35.34	38.48	29.66	29.06	37.15	38.71	37.35	42.13	33.85	44.47	26.82	29.18	36.74	34.45
Skilled manual	7.19	6.76	6.07	5.73	5.81	6.62	6.61	5.90	7.06	4.87	7.69	6.35	11.14	6.32	7.48	5.46
Partly skilled	16.20	15.96	16.94	13.12	14.83	17.21	30.23	19.89	31.47	20.89	26.15	19.76	14.55	18.16	15.44	16.05
Unskilled	7.20	4.12	6.95	2.60	13.43	5.46	4.39	2.67	2.06	3.11	6.15	1.41	6.36	1.54	4.91	3.58
N	176,034	293,369	2,043	3,802	499	2,161	2,299	5,355	340	1,417	65	425	440	1,107	1,671	4,923

Source: 1991 and 2001 Census, SARs. © Crown copyright